ACROSS THE
ATLANTIC

ACROSS THE
ATLANTIC

A BOY'S JOURNEY FROM
GHANA TO AMERICA

KWASI ACHEAMPONG

Published by Victorious You Press™
Charlotte NC, USA

TITLE: ACROSS THE ATLANTIC
First Printed: 2025
Editor: Charmaine LaFondé
Cover Designer: Toyin Badrudeen
ISBN: 978-1-959719-48-9
ISBN: (eBook) 978-1-959719-49-6
Library of Congress Control Number: 2025904911

Printed in the United States of America

For details email joan@victoriousyoupress.com
or visit us at www.victoriousyoupress.com

Dedication

TO MY BELOVED WIFE

Scarlett Acheampong, my partner, my confidante, and my compass. Your patience, strength, and grace fuel my spirit. Thank you for always standing by me, for believing in my dreams, and for helping me become the man I am. This journey would be impossible without you.

TO MY CHILDREN

Leon, Kyrie, and Nova, may you know that every word in these pages carries a piece of my heart and is written with you in mind. You fill my world with boundless energy, curiosity, and love. My hope is that you chase your dreams boldly, as you are the inspiration for every story I write.

TO MY LATE MOTHER

Ama Mensimah, your voice still echoes in my heart, your wisdom still guides my steps, and your love still nourishes my soul. Though you are no longer here, I feel you with me in everything I do. This book is as much yours as it is mine, a tribute to the lessons you instilled and the sacrifices you made. I am forever grateful for your strength, courage, and love.

TO ALL MY STUDENTS AT OUR BRIGHT FUTURE

This work is dedicated to you with profound love, respect, and gratitude. You are my foundation and my forever.

Contents

Introduction

Across the Atlantic: A Boy's Journey from Ghana to America is more than a simple account of migration; it's a tale of sacrifice, resilience, identity, and transformation inspired by the lives of those who crossed oceans and faced challenges to create new beginnings.

Follow the journey of a young boy from Ghana who, with his family of ten, left behind everything familiar for the unknowns of America. Through his eyes, you'll experience the challenges of adapting to a foreign land, the cultural clashes, and the strength that emerges when family bonds are tested.

Inspired by generations of immigrant stories and struggles, this book reflects a deep personal connection to that experience. Like many who've undertaken such journeys, the protagonist's story reflects the universal themes of hope, survival, and the quest for belonging.

Across the Atlantic is written for individuals who have undergone significant life transitions, those striving to connect by bridging the gap between two distinct worlds, or anyone who is intrigued by the essence and depth of the immigrant experience. Each chapter reveals the triumphs and setbacks and the moments of doubt and clarity that define the search for identity in a new land.

Thank you for joining me on this journey. Whether you've experienced a similar journey or simply wish to walk alongside those who have, I hope my story resonates with you.

CHAPTER 1
Leaving Ghana

April 22, 2000—etched in my mind like a prophecy—had finally arrived. It had been circled on our calendar for months as the day we would leave Ghana behind and step into the unknown promise of America. It wasn't just a date; it was destiny calling, a culmination of dreams, prayers, and endless hope. Everything in our lives had led to that moment, and the future was only a plane ride away.

Our local pastor, always kind, had offered to drive me, my mother, and my two younger brothers to Accra, the capital of Ghana. While in Accra, we stayed at the house of my mother's uncle—one of the few family members who had done well for himself. Our flight was scheduled to leave at 2:00 p.m., but since my uncle lived so close to the airport, the plan was to leave his house at noon.

When it was close to the time for us to leave, my mother's voice broke through the bustle: "Use the bathroom one more time before we go." I was overwhelmed by a mix of excitement and nerves as I obeyed, as always.

I entered the bathroom, closed the door, and did my business. When I tried to leave, the door wouldn't open. My heart skipped a beat; I jiggled the handle again—nothing. Panic started creeping in and I yanked harder, but the door stayed stubbornly shut. I yelled for my mother, and I heard her frustrated voice through the door, "Stop playing around and open it!" I couldn't.

Her uncle rushed over and tried to open the stuck door, but despite his efforts the door did not budge. With tension mounting, my uncle finally decided to call a locksmith, but the locksmith would not be able to arrive until 2:00 p.m. —the exact time our plane was scheduled to take off.

I crumpled to the cold bathroom floor in a torrent of tears. I had prayed so hard for the chance to leave, to start a new life in America. *Why is this happening to me now?* I thought; my faith was crumbling. My silent pleas to God for a miracle, a shift in circumstances, were met with nothing but deafening silence.

Through the door, I could hear my mother and her uncle talking in low, serious voices discussing options. I knew they were thinking they might have to leave me behind. Take my brothers and leave me. The mere thought of it shattered something deep within me. I was overwhelmed by a weight far beyond my years, leaving me feeling utterly helpless.

Then I heard my father's voice on the phone. He was calling from America, checking to see if we'd made it onto the plane. My mother's voice was heavy with disappointment as she explained the situation. I felt sick with shame that I had let my father down—I had let *everyone* down.

I curled up on the bathroom floor, sobbing until tears ceased to form. Time became a blur, and when the locksmith finally swung open the door, I felt little to no relief. I saw my mother's face drawn tight, as she told me we'd missed the plane and had to wait for my father's instructions. The silence in the house was suffocating. My mother, her uncle, my little brothers—they all looked at me with the same expression of disappointment. All I could do was collapse again, crying until the night swallowed me whole.

The next morning, I was jolted from a restless sleep by the piercing sound of my mother's voice. I quickly took my shower, with the bathroom door wide open daring it to trap me again. We dressed, piled into the car, and as the car rumbled down the road, tension was thick in the air. My mother's face was unreadable. She hadn't told us a thing—where we were going, what the plan was—and we knew better than to ask. Silence was our only option.

The car rumbled down the road, my mind racing with a thousand questions I couldn't voice. After thirty minutes, I heard a low roar in the distance. With every passing second, the sound became louder, and my heart leaped as I realized what it was. Planes!

I felt excitement well up inside me as I thought, *Could it really be happening? Could this finally be the moment we had been waiting for?* I nudged my younger brothers awake, and as soon as they heard the thunderous sound, they lit up with excitement. Their voices burst into song, filling the car with joyful chaos.

Tears welled up in my eyes as I joined them, our voices rising together in unison, singing in our native language (twi):

Da na se (Thanks)
Da na se (Thanks)
Da wo nyame na se (Thanks to God)
Da na se (Thanks)

Da na se (Thanks)
Da wo nyame na se (Thanks to God)
E fri se oye (Because he is good)
Da na do do so (And his goodness are many)
Da na se (Thanks)
Da na se (Thanks)
Da wo nyame na se (Thanks to God)

We were really doing it! Our dreams were about to take flight, and we were leaving for America! My heart swelled with a mix of disbelief and overwhelming joy. Vividly etched into my mind was the brilliant blue sky, streaked with wisps of white clouds as the sun bathed the city of Accra with a warm, golden glow.

"The plane is here!" shouted the pastor. My heart raced with anticipation as my brothers and I sprinted towards the waiting aircraft. The dusty ground stirred beneath our feet and our laughter, filled with excitement and nervous energy, echoed through the air. We skidded to a halt when our pastor's thunderous voice shouted "STOP!"

His expression was calm but firm. "Go give your mother a hug."

His words seemed absurd. I was ten, my brothers eight and seven. We exchanged glances, unsure whether to laugh or protest. According to our culture, the words of an elder were law, so with a mix of reluctance and obedience, we turned back. There stood our mother, tears brimming in her eyes. It never occurred to me, until that moment, that we were leaving our mother behind.

As she wrapped her arms around us in a desperate embrace, it was as if she were clinging to us for dear life. Her body trembled and her sobs grew heavier. Wiping her tears with my tiny little hands, my voice was steady and naïve. "Don't cry, Mama. We'll see you soon."

She nodded, forcing a smile through her anguish, but something in her eyes shattered me. To us, it was an adventure—a chance to finally be with our father, but as the years would later prove, my childhood innocence came face to face with a harsh reality. For my mother, it wasn't just a goodbye; it was an unimaginable sacrifice to let her children go in hopes we'd have a better life, even if it meant enduring the loneliness of our absence.

Let me take you back to where it all began—back to my humble beginnings.

CHAPTER 2
My Humble Beginnings

I grew up in a small village called Techiman, nestled in the Brong region of Ghana. Life was simple, but for a curious little boy like me, it was a world full of adventure and wonder.

My father, Edward Acheampong was a farmer, and my mother, Ama Acheampong made a living as a local fish dealer. Our bed was a simple carpet on the floor, but it felt like something out of a storybook to me—like Aladdin's magical flying carpet. We drank from the river or from the rain that collected after heavy storms, and although we didn't have much, we never considered ourselves to be poor. There is a popular saying, "it takes a village," and that was the reality of my childhood. By the time I was four or five, I could leave the house alone to play without a second thought. No one worried, because the entire community had their eyes on you. If a neighbor saw you misbehaving, they wouldn't hesitate to whip you, march you home, and explain exactly what you did wrong. Your parents would thank them and then whip you again just to make sure you learned the lesson. Discipline was everywhere. At school, if you were late, you were beaten. Got a question wrong? Beaten again. Oh, and because elders were never wrong, there was no room for questioning their authority.

For every African boy, soccer was our greatest joy—the heartbeat of our childhood. It was more than a game; it was how we bonded and built friendships. When the Ghana national team played, the whole country came alive. Businesses shut down and people either flocked to local bars or gathered around TVs to watch. If our team won, the streets exploded with celebration. We'd march together, singing and dancing in pure unity. As a little boy, I'd wake up early, grab my friends, and form teams to take on kids from neighboring areas. Our trophies were made of old, discarded cans we found on the streets. They weren't shiny cups or medals, but, to us, those cans were priceless treasures. Every victory felt like winning the World Cup, and every match was a story we carried in our hearts. Ghana was a place of pure happiness for me. That was life in Ghana—strict, simple, and full of joy, even in its roughest moments—and there *were* a few rough moments. One of those moments, involved my best friend, Yaw.

CHAPTER 3
Rain, River, Regret

Though Ghana was a place of joy, it also held dark shadows—moments that left scars. One day, I was out playing in the rain with my friends. The rain was falling in heavy sheets, drenching the earth, and turning everything into a slick, muddy playground. The river's edge became our soccer stadium, and the mud became our battlefield. As the ball splashed through puddles, waves of laughter echoed at every slip and every fall as we chased it. Struggling to keep our balance in the thick, wet mud, our clothes heavy with water and caked in dirt, the rain washed away any hint of scolding or chores waiting back home. For that brief, beautiful moment, we were untouchable—just kids, free and alive, playing as if the world belonged to us. Then the ball came to me.

My heart thundered in my chest as I trapped it with my foot. The slick mud made every movement a challenge. I glanced up and saw my best friend, Yaw, charging toward me, his grin as wide as the sky. With a quick fake to the left, I slipped past him, leaving him tumbling into the mud. There was nothing between me and the goal—a pair of rocks we'd placed on the riverbank to mark the goal posts. With the shouts of my friends urging me on, my pulse pounding in my ears, I leaned back and kicked the ball with everything I had, mud flying off my foot as it connected with the ball. The ball sailed wide, veering off course, and my heart sank as I watched it bounce twice before rolling into the swollen river.

Silence fell over us, broken only by the sound of the rain. We all froze, the rushing water roaring louder than ever as our only ball swept away instantly. My chest tightened with a mix of disappointment and guilt, but before any of us could stop him, Yaw—ever the fearless one—leaped into the river. "No, Yaw! Don't!" we all screamed, panic clawing at our throats. But Yaw was already in the water, cutting through the current with strong, confident strokes.

When Yaw reached the ball, a grin lit up his face. "See? Nothing to fear!" he shouted, throwing the ball back toward us as we all cheered. Ready to resume playing our muddy game, we heard Yaw's sharp and desperate cry. "Help! Help!"

Yaw's voice, once so bold and strong, was trembling with fear. I spun around to see him flailing in the river, his arms thrashing against the violent current. The rain-swollen river had become a monster, its currents dragging him deeper into its grip. We ran along the riverbank, our bare feet slipping in the thick mud, our shouts frantic and raw. "Yaw! Hold on!" We yelled, but his panicked eyes told us he couldn't.

As we followed him down the riverbank, we found and extended tree branches to him and shouted for him to grab hold. Our hearts sank as we helplessly watched each branch get caught in the violent flow and wash away. The rain mingled with tears on our faces as we stood there, powerless, watching the river swallow Yaw whole. Panic and guilt tore through me as we all ran home to get help. Afterall, I was the one who kicked the ball into the river. Through heaving breaths and tear-streaked faces, we told our parents the news. "Yaw's in the river! He's gone!"

The adults sprang into action, their faces pale with fear. The fire department was called, and soon flashing lights and frantic voices filled the riverbank. They searched for hours, combing through the rushing water, their flashlights cutting through the downpour as the rain finally eased. Ten blocks downstream, Yaw's body was pulled from the river, lifeless and still.

Seeing Yaw, who had once radiated vibrancy and laughter, now lying cold and silent, shattered something within each of us. He was rushed to the hospital, sirens wailing through the rain-soaked streets. We ran behind, our hearts pounding in our chests, praying, hoping, that somehow Yaw would make it. The minutes dragged on like hours, each second stretching painfully as we stood outside, numb and trembling, waiting for any word.

Finally, the doctor emerged. His face was unreadable, and the uncomfortable silence was unbearable. Then, as if to relieve the tension, he said, "He's alive. We've pumped most of the water out of his lungs. He's going to be okay."

A collective sigh of relief escaped our lips, and for the first time in hours, our fear was relieved. Yaw was alive! The next day, his entire group of friends came to visit. We were all eager to see him, to show him we had always been by his side.

With our faces all lit up with smiles, we walked into Yaw's room. He was sitting up in bed, his eyes open, but the familiar spark that used to shine in his eyes was gone. When we rushed to him, arms outstretched and eager to embrace him, he didn't move. He didn't smile. With a cold emptiness, he just stared at us, blank and unseeing. His face, once full of warmth and life, was distant, unfamiliar. Yaw didn't recognize us. Not even me.

It felt as if the room had shrunk around us. We stood there, frozen, caught between hope and confusion. His mother, who had been standing by the door, stepped forward, her face drawn with exhaustion and grief. "Come with me," she whispered, her voice thick with sorrow. We followed her into the waiting room, where she sat down, her hands trembling, and with a heavy sigh, she told us that Yaw had suffered a severe brain injury. Her words hit like a punch to the gut when she said the doctors weren't sure if he would ever regain his memory. We tried to hold it together, but it was impossible. With tear-filled eyes, Yaw's mother made a gentle appeal to each of us. "Please, don't come back," she said, her voice cracking. "He needs time. He needs space." We nodded, our hearts breaking for him—and for her.

I couldn't help but blame myself, the guilt gnawing at me, relentlessly. I could still see Yaw reaching out, his hands desperate to grab onto something, anything, as the current pulled him away. *If I hadn't kicked that ball so hard. If I had just made that shot. If I hadn't kicked the ball into the river, none of this would have happened.*

I haven't been able to trust any body of water since. Every time I try to swim or even dip my toes in, a wave of panic crashes over me. When I close my eyes, I see Yaw's face—his desperate eyes, his outstretched hands, grasping for something that wasn't there. No matter how calm or safe the water seems, all I see is the current pulling my best friend under, stealing him away. That moment is etched into the water itself, and no matter how hard I try, I can't escape it.

CHAPTER 4
Give it Time

We left the hospital, trying to process what we had just heard. With my heart shattered, I needed the comfort and wisdom I knew my Grandma Ada possessed. "Paa Kwasi," (my family nickname given by my grandmother) she said, wrapping me in a hug. "Give it time. Give Yaw's family space. They are going through so much. His elder sister is severely ill. You know that. Just give them time."

For years, Yaw's sister battled an illness no one could name. Her pain was a haunting melody that spilled through the thin walls of their home, her cries rising with the evening wind. Each night, she prayed aloud, begging God to take her, her words trembling with the desperation of a soul too weary to continue. Her suffering imprinted itself on the hearts of all who passed by her window, yet none felt it as deeply as Yaw.

While we were free to run through the schoolyard, laugh with friends, and lose ourselves in the carefree rhythm of childhood, Yaw didn't have that luxury. Every morning, as we packed our books and headed off to class, Yaw stayed behind. His world was not filled with lessons and games, but with quiet rooms and heavy responsibilities. His parents, worn thin by endless days of work to pay for medical bills, depended on him to stay home and care for his sister.

Yaw was her lifeline, carefully preparing her meals and coaxing her to eat when her pain robbed her of the will to try. He wiped her tears, whispered words of comfort when her cries filled the air, and held her hand throughout the nights that seemed to stretch on forever. His life revolved around her suffering, yet he bore it with a strength far beyond his years.

His devotion wasn't loud or boastful—it was steady and unyielding, a quiet rebellion against the hopelessness that tried to suffocate them all. While others looked away or surrendered to despair, Yaw stood firm, shouldering the burden with a grace that left even adults in awe.

Although Yaw and I were the same age, I looked up to him as if he were years ahead of me. His strength wasn't just physical, he carried burdens that would have crushed most people, yet he faced them with a quiet resilience that felt larger than life. Yaw was more than a friend—he was my hero.

Six months after the incident at the riverbank, the news came that Yaw had passed away. It felt like the ground beneath me had cracked open, his absence creating a void which was impossible to fill. The world seemed to dim in his absence, as the sharp, jagged, and constant ache of grief settled deep within my chest. One month later, Yaw's sister passed away. The pain from each loss was compounded, then came the whispers that chilled me to the core.

People spoke in hushed tones that Yaw's father had taken his daughter's life to end her suffering. The notion of a father making such an unthinkable decision continued to haunt me. It felt surreal, like a distorted tale no one should ever endure, yet it spread relentlessly.

CHAPTER 5
Grandma Ada, My Rock

Losing Yaw at such a young age was devastating, but my grandmother was my anchor; she was everything to me. When life got tough, she was the one who held me up, always knowing how to comfort me in the simplest yet most profound ways. She would cook my favorite dish, Baku, and I could never wait for it to be done. My hands were always in the pot, sneaking bites long before it was ready. She never said it outright, but I knew—I was her favorite.

She made sure I knew it in other ways, too, like when she slipped me three pieces of candy and whispered... "Paa Kwasi, one is for you, Daniel, and Kenny," she would say, passing treats to me. "I know it's tempting, so I'm giving you two extras, just in case."

One day, my mother had gone out to pick up her fish load, leaving us at home. The morning was calm until Uncle Allan showed up at our door. His face was tight, pale, and there was a look in his eyes that made my stomach twist. *"Grandma has passed away."*

For a moment, the world stopped. I froze, staring at him as if the force of my disbelief could undo his words. *No. He has to be lying.* My mind reeled—how could this be true? I was just with her yesterday. She had smiled, laughed. She couldn't be gone.

Before I knew what I was doing, I was running, my bare feet slapping the dirt road, wearing nothing but shorts. I didn't stop to grab a shirt or think about the heat or the rocks underfoot. Uncle Allan called after me, his voice urgent, but I tore away from him like a wild thing. I had to see her. She'd be there—I knew it. She *had* to be.

As I neared my grandmother's house, I slowed, confused by the crowd gathered outside, their faces somber, voices low, as if the air itself had grown heavier. My aunts and uncles were there, clustered together, their shoulders shaking with silent sobs. The sound of mourning hit me like a wave, yet I still didn't understand. *Why are they crying?* "Where is Grandma?" I asked. No response.

I stood there, trembling, my voice barely above a whisper as I asked again, "Where is Grandma?" My words hung in the air, desperate and raw, still—no one answered me. My aunts and uncles averted their eyes, their silence more crushing than any words could have been. Finally, one of my aunts stepped forward and wrapped her arms around me in a warm and tight embrace. I stood frozen in her grasp, unable to move and unable to cry. My mind was overtaken by a storm of disbelief and questions. *There's no way this is real. There's no way God would take my best friend and my grandmother in the same year. How could He?* Anger and betrayal crept in, and I started questioning everything I thought I understood about God and about life. *Why her? Why now?* The love and comfort she gave me, the warmth of her presence—it had always felt eternal. That it could just vanish was unbearable.

That night, I lay in bed, staring into the dark, unable to sleep. My mind raced with memories—her laughter, the sound of her voice, the way she always made me feel safe. In that moment, those memories felt so distant, like they belonged to someone else's life. Morning came, and I found myself drawn back to her house, clinging to some fragile hope that perhaps it was a mistake. In my heart, I was hoping that maybe she'd be there, sitting in her favorite spot, smiling like always.

The silence of the house was deafening. The space that had once been alive with her love and laughter felt hollow. The emptiness hit me like a tidal wave as the dam inside me broke. Tears poured from my eyes, uncontrollable and hot, and I screamed, "Where is my grandma? Where is my grandma?" My voice cracked with the weight of my grief until the truth settled in my chest like a stone. There were no cell phones then, so when my mother returned home the next day, she walked through the door smiling. Her expression shifted to confusion when she saw our faces, and then, breaking her silence, she sank to her knees, clutching her chest, and sobbed like a child. Watching her crumble was almost worse than my own grief. I felt powerless, a boy trying to make sense of a shattered world. I went to her, knelt beside her, and wrapped my arms around her. "I love you," I whispered over and over, but the words felt hollow, like they could never be enough to ease her pain or mine. Nothing could. Following Grandma Ada's death, a profound emptiness remained.

CHAPTER 6
Uncle Sam's Plan

M y uncle Sam, a Roman Catholic priest, was a man unlike any other in our family. His vocation connected him deeply to his faith, but also opened doors that most of us could only dream of. As a priest, he had the rare privilege of traveling the world, representing his parish and embracing opportunities that extended far beyond the small village where he and his siblings were born. Uncle Sam's life was filled with stories of places we'd only heard about in books or through whispered dreams—Rome, Paris, London—and one of those places was America.

It was love at first sight when Uncle Sam first set foot in America. The sprawling cities, the boundless opportunities, the promise of a life that seemed freer and fuller—it all captivated him. He believed that America wasn't just a place; it was a promise, one that could transform his family's future. Uncle Sam, being the most successful and educated of his siblings, felt a profound responsibility for everyone's well-being. His accomplishments weren't solely his own; they reflected the sacrifices of his parents and the shared dreams they all carried. His family leaned on him, not out of selfishness, but out of necessity. He was their rock, their hope.

Ever the problem-solver and visionary, Uncle Sam devised a bold plan that would pave the way for a brighter future for his siblings.

One by one, he would bring them to America. The plan was deceptively simple in its brilliance. He would start by bringing one sibling over—a seed of change. Once the first sibling was established, that sibling would, in turn, take on the responsibility of bringing the next sibling to America. It was a domino effect, fueled by sacrifice and trust. Each sibling would carry the weight of the other, like a relay race where the baton wasn't just hope, but the promise of a better life.

Due to immigration laws, Uncle Sam knew executing his plan would be challenging. He understood the financial strain that moving to America would bring and the emotional toll his family would face in leaving everything behind. Yet, his faith--in God and in his family--was unwavering. To him, America wasn't just an opportunity; it was a calling, a place where his family could flourish, unshackled from the limitations of their homeland.

His determination was unshakable, and soon, the wheels were in motion. Uncle Sam didn't just dream of change; he made it happen, one sibling at a time. And though the weight on his shoulders was immense, he carried it with grace, never letting the burden of his mission overshadow the love he had for his family.

Everything had been running like clockwork, just as Uncle Sam envisioned. One by one, each family member was brought to America. The plan was meticulous, a chain of sacrifices and responsibilities, and for a while, it seemed unstoppable—until it was my father's turn.

When it was my father's turn to move to America, he decided he couldn't follow the plan as it had been laid out. He refused to bring just one sibling or even just one person. Instead, he declared that he would bring his wife and all ten of his children with him. His decision was bold, to say the least, but it was also a logistical nightmare. It upended everything!

CHAPTER 7
The Edward Curse

The delicate balance that Uncle Sam had so carefully maintained came crashing down, sending ripples of shock and frustration through the family. My father's siblings felt betrayed, blindsided by what they saw as a selfish and reckless move. They accused my father of jeopardizing the careful system that had been their lifeline to a new world. Immigration processes were already challenging enough for one person at a time—what my father proposed was not only disrupting the system, but it was almost impossible to accomplish. The reaction from the family was swift and sharp, but my father refused to back down. He believed with every fiber of his being that his wife and children were meant to stay together, and the idea of leaving even one behind was unimaginable. For my father, keeping his immediate family united was a sacrifice worth any cost, even if it meant straining the relationships with his siblings.

The conflict quickly escalated, fracturing relationships within the family that had once seemed unbreakable. Uncle Sam, who had been the architect of their collective dream, found himself in the middle of a storm he hadn't foreseen as accusations flew back and forth. According to my stepmother, my father's decision caused a spiritual rift within the family and was the beginning of what she called the "Edward Curse." Was my father truly cursed by his family, or was it the natural consequence of a man who had chosen to stand alone, even against those who had once stood by him? My stepmother believed my father's siblings cursed him because of the darkness that followed him, alienating him from the rest of his family. She was convinced that my father pushed away so many of his loved ones, one by one, until he found himself almost entirely alone. I used to dismiss the idea of a curse as superstition, but as I grew older, I couldn't ignore the trail of broken relationships that seemed to stretch behind my father. Whatever the truth, my father's choice left scars—on him, on his siblings, and on the legacy of the American dream plan that had once seemed unshakable.

Polygamy is deeply rooted in Ghanaian tradition, often tied to the notions of wealth, family legacy, and societal standing. For many men, having multiple wives is seen as a symbol of their ability to provide for and grow an expansive family. My father embraced this cultural norm wholeheartedly, building a family that was as large as it was complex.

With four wives, my father's household was a mosaic of personalities and dynamics. Between them, he had ten children, each with their own unique place in the tapestry of our sprawling family. The eldest, Kent, was my half-brother—a natural leader with a quiet, serious demeanor. Then came Kevin, another half-brother, whose playful spirit often brought levity to tense situations. Next was Marcy, my half-sister, who possessed an uncanny ability to command attention wherever she went, whether through her sharp wit or her undeniable charm.

Following Marcy was Kyle, another half-brother, known for his rebellious streak that often left the family both exasperated and amused. Ava, my half-sister, was the dreamer of the family, her head often filled with ideas that seemed larger than life. Then came Alice, another half-sister, whose gentle, nurturing nature made her a cornerstone of support for all of us.

And then there was me—Kwasi. The seventh child and the second born to my father's fourth wife, I often felt like the bridge between my siblings. My perspective as both an observer and a participant in the chaos shaped me. My full brother Daniel followed, just two years younger than me, and we shared an unspoken bond that only brothers born from the same mother and father could truly understand.

Kenny, another half-brother, brought boundless energy and a mischievous grin to every room he entered, always ready to stir things up, and finally, there was Joy, born in 2003, my full sister and the youngest of us all. As the baby of the family, Joy's arrival seemed to mark a new chapter, one that carried both hope and the weight of all that had come before her.

Our family wasn't just large—it was layered, with each sibling navigating their own identity while trying to find their place in the shifting dynamics of our father's household. The presence of multiple mothers added another level of complexity. Alliances formed, misunderstandings brewed, and yet, at the heart of it all, there was an unbreakable thread of shared blood and history. We didn't always get along—how could we, in such a large and multifaceted family? But in moments of unity, we were a force to be reckoned with.

For my father, his family wasn't just a source of pride; it was a legacy, a testament to his belief in the strength of numbers and the importance of kinship. But it also meant navigating the delicate balance of keeping peace among four wives and ten children, each with their own needs, dreams, and challenges. It was a task that sometimes seemed impossible, but my father took it on with the same determination that defined his entire life.

My father arrived in New York in 1996, driven by the hope of building a better future for himself and his family. New York was nothing like the village he had left behind in Ghana—it was loud, fast-paced, and filled with opportunities that seemed endless if you could work hard enough to seize them. My father threw himself into his new world, working tirelessly to establish a foothold.

By 1998, my father had begun the process of reuniting with his third wife and his two eldest children, Kent and Kevin. It was a slow and grueling endeavor, with paperwork, legal obstacles, and financial constraints that seemed to stretch endlessly, but my father dreamed of the day when all ten of his children could stand together on American soil, ready to embrace a future full of promise. Everything was moving forward until my father's mother passed away. With her death, the foundation of my father's plans began to shift.

We only visited my father's parents on holidays, so I barely knew them. In the wake of the loss of my father's mother, rumors began to spread like wildfire through our family and community back in Ghana that my father might be coming back. Some said he was overwhelmed with grief and unable to handle the weight of being so far from home when the matriarch of his family passed. Others whispered that he felt his place was back in Ghana, where he could reconnect with his roots and honor her memory. Whatever the reason, the uncertainty of his return created a ripple of anxiety and anticipation for all of us.

I was only six years old when my father left Ghana for America, too young to understand the full weight of his departure. I didn't know what it meant for him to leave his children and wives behind, nor could I grasp the sacrifices he was making for a future we couldn't yet see. In his absence, he became more of an idea than a person—a name spoken in conversations, a figure in the stories my family told, someone I admired from afar but didn't truly know.

When I heard the rumors that he might be coming back, a wave of excitement and anxiety crashed over me. After two long years, the thought of seeing him again felt both thrilling and terrifying. I barely remembered what it was like to have him around. Would he recognize me? Would I recognize him?

His presence—or the lack of it—had shaped my life in ways I couldn't yet understand, but as the possibility of his return loomed, it felt like everything was about to change.

The journey would take two days, but for a child waiting for a father he hadn't seen in years, it might as well have been an eternity. My thoughts circled endlessly, a restless storm of joy and uncertainty.

On the second day, just before sunset, I heard the sound of tires crunching over the dusty road that led to our home. A sleek, private car, a rare sight in our village, parked outside our house felt almost surreal, like something out of a story. My heart raced as I sprinted to the front door to get a better look.

The car door opened, and I saw my mother step out first, her expression glowing with exhaustion and excitement. Before I could stop myself, I ran to her, throwing my arms around her waist and burying my face in her side. She laughed, stroking my head gently. "Paa Kwasi," she said, her voice warm and teasing, "you see me every day. Go give your father a hug. It's him you've been waiting for."

Her words jolted me into action as I ran around the car, my bare feet kicking up little clouds of dust. My heart pounded as I rounded the vehicle, and saw my father stepping out of the car, unfolding his tall frame with an air of quiet dignity. For a moment, I just stood there, staring at him. He looked exactly as I'd imagined--like the image of him in my mind had suddenly come to life. I threw myself at him, my small arms wrapping tightly around his waist before he could fully straighten up. He froze for a split second, then let out a deep chuckle, the kind that seemed to resonate from his chest. He stood tall, lifting me off the ground with ease as I clung to him.

"Dad," I whispered, my voice trembling, "you're finally home." I buried my face in his shoulder, the fabric of his shirt rough against my skin, but I didn't care. I held on as tightly as I could, afraid that if I let go, he might disappear again.

His hand rested on the back of my head, steady and reassuring. "Paa Kwasi," he said softly, his voice deep and warm, "I'm home now. I'm here."

In that moment, everything else faded away. The years of distance, the rumors of his return, the anxiety and uncertainty—they all melted into the background. All that mattered was that my father was holding me like he'd never let go. As we stood there in the golden light of the setting sun, I felt a warmth I hadn't known I was missing. It was the feeling of family, of something whole, even if just for that moment.

My father's return brought a wave of joy that swept through our home, transforming it almost overnight. It wasn't just his presence—it was the way it ignited a spark in each of us. My mother, who had carried so much of the family's burden in his absence, seemed to radiate happiness. Her smile came more easily, her laughter filled the air, and her energy lifted us all. In Ghanaian culture, they say a woman is the temperature of the home, and when she is happy, the whole house thrives. My father's return had brought her warmth back, and with it, a sense of harmony that had been missing for years.

Though my pain of Grandma Ada's absence still lingered, my father's return made the pain a little easier to bear. It felt like the family was healing, slowly but surely. In our community, when a father comes home from America, it's more than a family reunion—it's a symbol of achievement, almost like striking gold. My father had been to the land of opportunity, and now he had come back to us, bringing with him the promise of better days, and he didn't come back empty-handed. No, my father returned with treasures that felt like dreams come true for kids like us. Among his gifts were bicycles—real, gleaming bicycles. In our neighborhood, bicycles were more than toys; they were status symbols, the kind of thing other children could only imagine owning. We couldn't believe our luck. Riding those bikes down the dusty roads, we felt invincible, like kings and queens in a kingdom of our own making. The stares from other kids, the whispered envy—it all made us feel like we were on top of the world.

But it wasn't just the material things that mattered. It was the way my father's presence shifted the air in our home. He brought with him a sense of stability and reassurance that we hadn't even realized we were missing. One memory stands out above all the rest, etched into my heart like a cherished photograph. We were all piled into my father's car, me sandwiched between my brothers, Daniel and Kenny, in the back seat. My parents sat in the front, their voices weaving together in conversation, their laughter spilling over like music. The radio was playing softly in the background, and a popular song came on, one that everyone in Ghana seemed to know by heart.

The song was triumphant, a celebration of someone who had "made it." My father's face lit up as he began singing along, his voice rich and full of pride. He tapped the steering wheel in rhythm, the lyrics flowing from him as if he had written them himself. My mother turned to him, her eyes shining with pride and adoration. She didn't sing; she simply watched him, her smile gentle but unwavering, as if she were capturing the moment, preserving that version of him to treasure forever.

I sat in the back, watching them. Their love wasn't loud or showy—it was steady, like a current running beneath the surface of everything. In that moment, I didn't just see my parents, I saw partners, two people who had weathered storms together and come out stronger. A silent wish formed in my young heart. I wanted to know what it felt like to love someone like that and to be loved in return. To share a connection so deep and joyful that it could light up a car ride, a home, an entire life. Watching them, I realized that their love wasn't just for them—it spilled over into all of us, filling the spaces that had once felt empty.

Just as quickly as he had brought joy and renewal to our home, it was time for my father to leave. He stayed for a month—thirty short days that felt like a fleeting moment in time. When the day came for him to return to America, a heaviness settled in my chest, as if someone had placed a stone there that I couldn't shake off.

At the airport, we stood as a family, clinging to every last second with him. My siblings and I crowded around, desperate to make the most of his presence while we still had it. He hugged each of us tightly, his embrace filled with unspoken promises. When it was my turn, I wrapped my small arms around him and squeezed as hard as I could, as though holding on tight enough might somehow make him stay.

He knelt down to meet my eyes, his hands firm on my shoulders. "Paa Kwasi," he said with a soft smile, "I'll be back. And soon, you'll all come to America with me. We'll be together again—I promise."

I nodded, swallowing the lump in my throat, and watched as he straightened up, kissed my mother on the cheek, and turned toward the boarding gate. We stood there, waving, as the engines of the plane roared to life. I felt a pang of sadness watching him go, the silhouette of my father disappearing into the crowd, but I held on tightly to his words. He had promised, and my father was my hero. In my heart, I believed he would not let us down.

True to his promise, my father started the process to bring the next group of siblings: Marcy, Kyle, Ava, and Alice, to America. Watching them prepare to leave was bittersweet. On one hand, it felt like a victory, but on the other, it deepened the ache as I stood on the sidelines, waving them off with a mixture of pride and envy, silently counting down the days until it would be my time to go.

CHAPTER 8
My Mother: Ama

When my mother, Ama, was just 17 years old, her world was turned upside down. My grandmother, Ada, who had been the pillar of her family, was suddenly disabled by illness and no longer able to work. In an instant, my mother's role in the family took a dramatic turn. What should have been the prime of her adolescence became the beginning of a life of relentless sacrifice and responsibility. Forced to drop out of school, she took on the daunting task of raising her younger siblings while simultaneously stepping into my grandmother's role as the family breadwinner. The dry fish business, once the lifeline of their household, rested squarely on her shoulders. It was no small burden for a teenager, but my mother approached it with determination and grit far beyond her years.

Every morning before dawn, my mother rose, hands raw from cleaning fish, body aching from the day before. Balancing heavy baskets on her head, she navigated uneven paths to the bustling market—a chaotic battleground of shouts, smells, and relentless bargaining. Selling fish wasn't just business; it was survival. With sharp wit and unyielding resolve, she commanded respect, holding firm against low offers and mastering quick negotiation. Every coin earned carried the weight of our family's survival, shaping her not just as a seller, but as a strategist in both business and life.

The income she earned went toward food, school fees for her siblings, and medical expenses for her mother. At night, despite her feelings of exhaustion, she prepared meals, helped her siblings with their studies, and whispered words of encouragement to keep their spirits high.

My mother was more than a provider; she was our source of hope and stability, even when hers had been interrupted. She had a natural aptitude for numbers, a gift she quickly realized was vital in the competitive and often ruthless environment of the market. "I learned math through counting money," she would often say with a wry smile. Calculations came as naturally to her as breathing, and she developed an innate ability to spot discrepancies and opportunities alike.

The fish business was a man's world, dominated by seasoned vendors and sharp negotiators who saw young women like her as easy targets, but my mother was no easy prey. She understood that mastery over numbers and the intricate workings of the trade was her armor against deceit. She kept meticulous records, never allowing a single coin to go unaccounted for. Her sharp eyes missed nothing, and her quick wit ensured no one dared to shortchange her. "They can smell fear in the market," she once told me, "But they also smell confidence—and I made sure they smelled mine."

My grandmother, Ada, a formidable woman in her own right, bore nine children, while my grandfather fathered an astonishing 42. A respected village chief and devout Muslim, my grandfather had seven wives, each contributing to a family tree so vast that my mother sometimes joked about its absurdity.

"I could pass some of my half-siblings on the street and not recognize them," she would laugh, a blend of amusement and resignation in her voice.

My grandmother, originally a Methodist, converted to Islam upon marrying my grandfather, diligently embracing the faith. My mother and all her siblings were raised in the Islamic faith, their upbringing steeped in the teachings and traditions that guided their family's daily life. For my mother, faith was both a source of strength and a constant reminder of the interconnectedness of her large family.

Life in such an expansive household came with its challenges. Resources were often stretched thin, and the dynamics between the wives and their children were far from simple. Yet, my mother's resilience and intellect allowed her to navigate these complexities with grace. She learned to adapt, read people, and find her place amidst the intricate web of relationships. Those experiences shaped her ability to lead with wisdom and pragmatism, qualities that would later define her not only as a sister and daughter but as a woman and mother.

The combination of her sharp mind, unshakable resolve, and ability to find humor in even the most overwhelming circumstances made her truly extraordinary. She created a place for herself and her siblings in a world that demanded so much of her and gave so little in return.

When my mother left her mother's home to carve her own path, she made a bold and defining choice—she embraced Christianity, adopting the Pentecostal denomination with the same passion and determination she brought to every aspect of her life. While it was a deeply personal decision, it was one her mother wholeheartedly supported. My grandmother, despite her own devout Islamic faith, encouraged my mother to follow her heart and seek the spiritual path that resonated most deeply with her. Years later, inspired by her unwavering conviction and the transformation they saw in her life, many of her siblings followed her lead, choosing to also adopt Christianity as their faith.

Faith became a cornerstone of my mother's identity, shaping her approach to every challenge she faced. Her devotion to her new faith was not passive—it was an active, driving force that inspired her to push forward, even in the face of insurmountable odds. It wasn't just something she practiced; it was something she lived, infusing every action with purpose, every struggle with hope, and every victory with gratitude.

A tireless worker, my mother was known for her almost superhuman energy and determination. Her siblings, in moments of playful admiration, would teasingly say she worked like a man, and they weren't wrong—her work ethic was unparalleled. She had tasted the bitterness of having nothing and was resolute in her mission to create a better life for her children. For her, failure was not an option, and no task was beneath her. Whether she was laboring in the fields, negotiating fiercely in the marketplace, or stretching a meager budget to feed seven mouths, she gave it everything she had. When my father left for America with his third wife and two older children, the full weight of raising seven children fell upon my mother. Like most children, we tested boundaries, demanded more than she could give, and often failed to see the enormity of her sacrifices.

She never complained though the weight of her responsibilities was visible in the lines etched into her face and the weariness in her eyes. She carried the burden with grace, channeling her frustration and fatigue into determination.

There were moments of anger and exhaustion, yes, but also moments of laughter and tenderness, of storytelling and wisdom shared over simple meals. She gave us everything she had—her time, her energy, and her unwavering belief that we could rise above our circumstances.

It was one of those days when the sun hung heavy in the sky, and the chores seemed endless. My mother had sent us, as she often did, to the river to fetch water for drinking, cooking, and bathing. The task was as routine as breathing for us, but on that particular day, I felt the itch of rebellion. I didn't want to haul those heavy buckets back home. I wanted to feel the freedom of the wind in my face and the thrill of doing something—anything—that wasn't work.

Without a second thought, I bolted, leaving my siblings standing dumbfounded on the riverbank. My legs carried me faster than they could react, and their calls to stop quickly faded behind me. I felt triumphant in those fleeting moments, the thrill of defiance coursing through me.

By the time I reached what I thought was a safe distance, panting and grinning with self-satisfaction, a stranger appeared in my path. I froze, startled and confused. With a firm but amused expression, the stranger informed me that my mother had paid him to track me down. My heart sank. She had outsmarted me, yet again. When I was marched back to the house, my mother stood waiting, her arms crossed and her face a mix of disappointment and resolve. She didn't say much—she didn't need to; her silence spoke volumes. She was resourceful, creative, and relentless when it came to ensuring that her children learned responsibility, respect, and the value of hard work, teaching us that actions have consequences.

Sacrificing her position as sister, playmate, or equal, she became her siblings' anchor, disciplinarian, teacher, and, in many ways, their surrogate mother. At first, they resented her authority, seeing her not as a sister, but as an extension of the hardships they were enduring. She was the one who enforced rules, handed out punishments, and demanded responsibilities that sometimes felt unfair to their young hearts.

"Someday, you'll thank me," she would say quietly, her voice heavy with the weight of her responsibilities. As they grew older, her siblings recognized the depth of her sacrifices. She had given up her childhood, her dreams, and her education to make sure they had food to eat, clothes to wear, and a chance to go to school. The younger ones, who once saw her as strict and unyielding, grew to admire her strength and selflessness. They leaned on her wisdom and sought her guidance, acknowledging that her sacrifices had paved the way for their own opportunities. My mother often reflected on how she missed being just a sister, someone who could laugh, cry, and share secrets without the weight of responsibility between them. But she accepted the change with grace, knowing she had done what was necessary.

My mother had always dreamed of a better life for us, one where we wouldn't know the same hardships that had shaped her existence. She wanted us to have opportunities that went beyond the confines of her world, chances to dream bigger than she ever could. Knowing that did not make it easier when the day arrived for us to leave. She felt as though a piece of her heart had been torn away, and she felt the ache of our absence for days after we had left for America. The house was quieter, and emptier, without the noise and chaos of children. But her love was vast, as wide as the ocean that now separated us. In her heart, she silently promised us the same thing she had promised her siblings years before: that she would do whatever it took to give us a better chance at life. Her sacrifice wasn't just about letting us go; it was about trusting that the values she had instilled in us—the resilience, the faith, the determination—would carry us forward.

Although my mother struggled with the loneliness and the fear that comes with letting go, my mother's story is one of love that transcends distance. Her story reveals the strength of a mother who was the foundation for every step her children took toward their own brighter tomorrows.

CHAPTER 9
Arriving in America

On April 24, 2000, at 9:45 a.m., our plane arrived in New York. My heart raced as I spotted my father, stepmother, and all my half-siblings eagerly waiting for us. They couldn't possibly miss us in our bright orange African dashikis, vibrant against the backdrop of the city. Finally, we made it to America. I was reunited with my father and siblings, and it felt surreal. As I stared out the window, my eyes widened in wonder at the towering buildings of New York, each one a giant reaching for the sky. In my naïve mind, I believed my father was rich. After all, he had brought a private car and bicycles back to Ghana. As we made our way to Webster, Massachusetts, I gazed at the apartment buildings of the complex and thought, *Wow, my father owns all these buildings.* We stopped in front of building 14, and when we stopped, I felt a mix of anticipation and confusion. *Why were we stopping there?* I held tightly to my childhood fantasy as we stepped into the modest three-bedroom basement apartment, with bunk beds crammed closely together. I clung to the illusion that we were only there for the night, but reality soon hit me; my father was not the wealthy man I imagined. Despite the circumstances, there was a wave of happiness that we finally had our first bed.

My father worked two jobs: one at a nursing home for the elderly assisting the certified nursing assistants, and the other at a group home, caring for adults with significant disabilities. My stepmother labored at a TJ Maxx factory. They were hard workers and had to rely on each other. My two little brothers, Daniel and Kenny, were always my responsibility. Whether we walked to and from school or played outside, I was their protector, their guide in our strange new world. The transition to a new life, new culture, and new expectations was like being thrown into a storm without warning. At the heart of it all, what we wanted most wasn't a new house, new clothes, or new toys— we longed for the familiar comfort of our mother's voice. As Daniel and I adjusted to our new life in America, one of the most painful realities we faced was watching our half-siblings reconnect with their mother. Their bond, once distant, seemed to flourish in a way that left us feeling even more isolated. We watched them laugh together, share stories, and enjoy the simple comforts of her presence. The sight of them being mothered—truly and physically—stirred a longing in us that we couldn't ignore.

Every hug they received, every meal she lovingly prepared, and every moment spent basking in her affection was a painful reminder of what we had left behind in Ghana. Daniel and I would sit silently, observing their interactions, as the ache within us grew deeper. It wasn't jealousy—it was more of a longing, an unspoken desire to have what they had—the presence of their mother. We missed our mother so much it felt like salt on an open wound, seeing our half-siblings with their mother only made our wound sting more. After begging, pleading, and crying; asking to speak to our mother, we were allowed to speak to her. Whenever we connected, the same question would escape my lips almost instinctively: *"When are you coming to America?"* It didn't matter how many times she reassured me that she loved us, all I wanted was her presence. She assured me, each time we called, that she was doing what was best for us and that she missed us as much as we missed her, but I missed the warmth of her arms, the safety of her gaze, and the reassurance that everything would be okay. After a month or two of countless calls to my mother, the phone calls ended. My father believed the transition into our new lives would somehow be much easier if we focused on adjusting to our new home, but, to me, it felt like my world was being ripped apart all over again. One day, I had my mother's voice, her promises, and her love—then suddenly, I had nothing. Days turned into endless weeks without me hearing from the one who had been my protector, my guide, and my anchor. I did not hear my mother's voice again until I was eighteen years old!

My mother's absence from my life for those eight long years left a mark on me—a wound that didn't bleed but festered deep inside. I felt abandoned, as though she had chosen something else over me. I was too young to understand the depth of her sacrifice or the unbearable pain she must have felt letting us go. All I knew was that the mother who had held me close through every scrape and heartbreak had become an unreachable figure on the other side of an ocean. I could not articulate my feelings of abandonment, but the trauma caused me to become quiet and withdrawn. I retreated into myself in ways that even I didn't fully understand. At school, I felt like a ghost, floating through the hallways without being seen or understood. While other kids laughed and made friends, I kept my head down, unsure of how to bridge the gap between their world and mine.

At home, I struggled to connect with my father and stepmother. Though they provided for me, it wasn't the same as the nurturing love I had known from my mother. The absence of her warmth left me feeling like I was drifting, unmoored, and uncertain of where I belonged. Daniel and I clung to each other, but even that bond couldn't fill the void her absence created.

School was another challenge altogether. In Ghana, we spoke proper English, a remnant of our colonial past under British rule. It took nearly two years to catch on to American slang, which felt like a foreign language. The American kids were not the kindest; they teased me mercilessly. I remember one boy approaching me and asking if I was gay. In Ghana, I had been taught that "gay" meant joyful, so I answered with a cheerful, "Yes!" They erupted into laughter, and I felt the sting of embarrassment wash over me like ice water. I went home that day with a heavy heart, asking my older sisters what "gay" meant. They explained that in America, it referred to a boy liking another boy. That was the first time I had ever encountered such a concept, and I was filled with confusion and questions after that encounter. It was not easy for me to step out of the isolation I'd wrapped myself in, but little by little, I began to forge friendships. I found small openings to connect, and one of my first friends was Maria.

CHAPTER 10
Friendship in a Foreign Land

Maria lived in our apartment complex (Southside), and one afternoon, during recess, she invited me to join her in a game of tag. She was a couple of years older and had a quiet, understanding nature that made me feel at ease. I hadn't felt that way in months, but on that day, for the first time in what felt like forever, I felt seen and included. The buzz of excitement from the day carried me home like a wave. I raced into the apartment, my face lit up with joy, and announced to my siblings, who were sprawled out in the living room, "I'm going to play with my friend!" My siblings all looked at me as if I'd grown six heads, but their surprised expressions didn't dampen my excitement. They could see how much the moment meant to me, and none of them questioned me. Without wasting a second, I made my way to Maria's building and eagerly buzzed her apartment. "Who is it?" came her voice through the intercom, calm and measured. "Kwasi!" I replied, my voice trembling with nervous anticipation. She buzzed me in, and I sprinted up the stairs, my heart pounding as I imagined the fun we were about to have.

When I knocked on her door, there was no immediate answer. I knocked again, and after what felt like an eternity, the door finally creaked open. Maria peeked out; her face shadowed with worry. Her expression caught me off guard, but I was too excited to think much of it.

"I wanted to see if you could come outside and play," I said eagerly. Maria hesitated, glancing nervously over her shoulder. "Okay, hold on," she finally said, her voice soft and uneasy. Something about her hesitation piqued my curiosity, and before I could think better of it, I gently pushed the door open a little wider with my foot and stepped inside.

"Wait, Kwasi—" Maria began, but it was too late. My feet had already carried me into the kitchen. I saw a woman slumped over the kitchen table, her face was slack, and she was not moving. Her arm was tied off with a piece of fabric, a needle still stuck into her skin. The room carried a faint scent of alcohol mixed with something sharp and unidentifiable. "Maria?" I said, my voice trembling. Before I could say more, she emerged from her room, her face a mask of concern. She froze for a moment when she saw where I was standing, then quickly stepped forward, taking my arm and steering me toward the door. My young mind couldn't fully process what I was seeing, but I knew something was deeply, deeply wrong.

"That's my mom," she said quietly, her voice taut with shame. "She's sick."

Maria didn't try to explain further, and I didn't ask. Somehow, even as young as I was, I understood it was something she didn't want to talk about. That day marked a shift in my understanding of the world. For the first time, I realized that everyone had their own struggles, their own silent battles hidden behind closed doors. Maria became more than just a friend to me after that—she became someone I admired, not for her strength alone, but for her resilience in the face of a life that was clearly much harder than I'd imagined.

Southside was more than just a low-income housing complex; it was a world unto itself, filled with contradictions that were as stark as they were unavoidable. On the surface, it was a place where hope and hardship lived side by side. Rent was based on income and the state subsidized housing for most of the residents. Many of the people who landed there were recovering addicts fresh out of rehab, given a second chance by a system that hoped proximity to others in the same situation might foster community and accountability. But in reality, having so many people with fragile hopes and fractured pasts crowded into one place often created an explosive environment.

Tensions ran high, and fights were a regular occurrence. Addiction haunted the hallways like a ghost that refused to leave. Arguments over money, drugs, or simply the pressures of life would escalate, sometimes spilling out into the courtyards for everyone to witness. Still, amidst the chaos, there were glimmers of resilience. Some neighbors banded together, creating small pockets of community where they supported one another in their struggles to reclaim their lives.

For my family, Southside wasn't just a place to live; it was where we learned the dualities of life—its ugliness and its beauty; its heartbreak and its hope. It shaped who we were, testing our strength every single day. We were surrounded by neighbors who knew what it meant to struggle and who understood the fine line between hope and despair because they lived it every day.

But as much as Southside built us, it also broke us in ways that weren't immediately visible. As I grew older, I began to see how deeply the environment we lived in could pull people down. By the age of twelve, I watched friends succumb to the temptations that surrounded us. Weed became the first step, almost a rite of passage for kids desperate to find their footing in an unsteady world. Then came selling, a quick way to make cash in a community where opportunities were scarce. Harder drugs—Percocet, cocaine, heroin—followed soon after, turning youthful experimentation into dangerous addictions.

The pressure to join in was constant. Saying no wasn't just a choice, it was an act of rebellion against the current of the world we lived in. It was easier to go along with the crowd, to give in to the promises of quick relief or fast money, but I knew the cost was far too high. I had dreams—dreams that stretched beyond the confines of Southside. I wanted to go to college, to play soccer at a professional level, and to turn my passion into a future. Drugs were a dead end, and I couldn't afford to let them extinguish the fire I carried within me.

But my dreams weren't just about me. I had younger brothers who looked up to me, and who needed me to be more than just an older sibling. Southside didn't have room for mistakes, not when one bad decision could mean a lifetime of regret. I took on the role of protector, not because I wanted to, but because I had to. "If I ever catch you doing drugs, I swear I'll kill you," I told them once, my voice hard with conviction. The words felt strange coming out of my mouth. They weren't the words of a brother—they were the words of a father, a role I had stepped into without realizing it.

The weight of that responsibility was heavy, but it was also what kept me grounded. I couldn't afford to slip, not when they were watching my every move, learning from my choices. Southside challenged us in ways I wouldn't fully grasp until much later, but even in the darkest times, I clung to the hope that something better waiting for us on the other side. All I had to do was keep pushing forward, one step at a time.

CHAPTER 11
The Edward Curse Strikes Again

My father had already kicked out my two older brothers, Kent and Kevin. My stepmother and her oldest daughter, Marcy, tirelessly worked over 40 hours a week, only to hand over their hard-earned paychecks to my father. In return, he would give each of them a mere $20. Although my stepmother endured the humiliation, I often overheard conversations she had with her children, tearfully lamenting the insult of receiving the same amount as her daughter. They encouraged her to voice her grievances to my father, knowing that such a conversation might ignite his fury. On a Saturday afternoon, a rare occasion when my father was home, my stepmother seized that opportunity to confront my father. *How dare she question him about money!*

In Ghanaian culture, the father is traditionally the head of the household, and the primary provider, while the mother's role is to care for the family. In the eyes of my stepmother and half-sisters, that traditional structure had shifted, and the authority within the family had become more fluid. She spoke passionately to my father about fairness and suggested she keep her check and pay whatever bills he wanted her to manage. That conversation ignited a firestorm! An argument ensued and escalated with raised voices and heated emotions. I had never seen my father so enraged. In a desperate attempt to defend her mother, Marcy intervened, making matters worse. "Grab your things and get out of my house!" my father demanded. A child questioning their father was considered to be one of the highest forms of disrespect. That cultural belief defined how we navigated our roles within our family and the larger context of our culture.

I stood frozen, my heart aching as I watched my father forcibly drag Marcy out of the house, while my stepmother fell to her knees, tears streaming down her face, pleading with my father. Where would she go? We were immigrants in a strange land, with few connections or resources. Through her anguished cries, my stepmother pointed a trembling finger at me and Daniel and whispered words that cut deep: "He will do this to you too, mark my words." We watched in helpless silence as she wept throughout the night, her sobs echoing in my mind. I lay awake, the weight of uncertainty pressing down on me, haunted by questions that had no answers. Facing the saddest day of our lives in America, my stepmother's words weighed heavily on my mind for months. I finally gathered the courage to ask her, "Why didn't you point to your own kids when you told us that my father would do the same thing to us?" With a soft bitter laugh she said, "Oh, he'll do it to them too. I just wanted you to know that you're not exempt from his behavior." I didn't want to believe her; my father was still my hero—the man who had brought us bicycles in Ghana and kept his promise to bring us to America. She saw the doubt on my face and explained to me the darker side of what the family still referred to as the "Edward Curse."

Because my father had chosen to bring his wife and children to America instead of his siblings, his family had placed a curse on him—a curse that would make him slowly push away each of his loved ones, one by one. As she spoke, her words filled me with confusion and disbelief. I was too young to fully grasp it all, and she must have seen it on my face because she stopped and gently told me to go play.

What happened to Marcy was the calm before the storm. My stepmother never recovered from the day my father kicked out her firstborn daughter. The heartbreak of not knowing where her child was weighed on her every day, and when my father was not at home, my stepmother found a way to call around to check on Marcy's well-being. We weren't allowed to talk to her. She was out there, bouncing from one friend's couch to another until she finally managed to save enough to rent an apartment. I continued to hope our parents would figure things out, but instead, everything took a turn for the worse.

One Saturday afternoon, after getting home from a soccer game, I heard them fighting again, their voices booming from the bedroom. I was the only one home, so to avoid them, I decided to hop in the shower, hoping to leave before things got worse. As soon as I opened the bathroom door, my stepmother burst out of the bedroom, her face streaked with tears, screaming, "You hit me! You hit me!" I froze, unable to process what was happening. Before I could say a word, she turned to me, her eyes wild with rage, accusing me of standing there and watching it happen. I was stunned, lost in the chaos. I said nothing. I just slipped into my room, dressed as fast as I could, and left the house, trying to escape the nightmare that had unfolded. I kept the hurt and anger inside, but on that day, my father stopped being my hero.

That night, I sat silently as my stepmother demanded to know why I hadn't come to her rescue. I just shut down. The next day, my stepmother moved out, leaving behind, me, my brothers, Daniel and Kenny, and my sisters, Ava and Alice. My sisters were next—I knew it was only a matter of time.

CHAPTER 12
The Great Escape

I came home from school one day and could hear my sisters arguing from their room. Curious, I popped my head in to check on them. "Get out!" they shouted in unison. That was their go-to response whenever I interrupted.

"Is everything okay?" I asked, hesitating at the doorway.

"It's your dad again," Alice snapped. "He wants us each to pay $500 a month, or we can't live here anymore."

Their frustration was palpable. I could see it in their faces, in the tension filling the room. They were arguing about what to do—pay my dad, or take their $1,000 and find their own place, somewhere they could live without constantly being on edge. As much as I didn't want them to leave, I knew they were right. It was their chance to escape the madness that was consuming our home. The following month, they made their move.

My father came home late, around 11:30 p.m. As usual, he poked his head into our rooms to check on us. He looked into the boys' room first and we all pretended to be asleep. We knew what was coming next. He opened my sisters' door--silence--he flicked on the lights, and the truth hit him. Their room was empty. Everything was gone.

He stormed back into our room, shaking us awake. "Where are they?" he demanded, his voice cracking with panic. We played dumb, acting as if we had no idea what he was talking about. That was the first time I had ever seen my father cry. He called out for Alice mostly, his voice raw with grief (Alice was his favorite). She was the one who would always go out of her way for him. Even though he did not buy us anything for our birthdays, Alice always made sure there was a present in his room on his birthday. She'd put all our names on it, making it look like it was from everyone. That was Alice—selfless, kind-hearted, always thinking of others, even when they didn't deserve it. Alice, the one person who had held us all together, had left, and, at that moment, I realized just how fragile our family truly was.

I believe much of my father's outbursts and the deep-rooted trauma he carried stemmed from the loss of his family, especially in a foreign world that was nothing like the one he knew. He came to America with one goal: to work hard and provide a better life for us. He believed that if he worked tirelessly and dedicated himself to his job and his responsibilities, everything would eventually fall into place. What my father didn't realize, was that raising a family was far more complicated than just providing for basic needs; especially in a place that is so different from the place that was left behind.

Work, though essential, wasn't enough. You had to show love, you had to nurture, and you had to be there emotionally as much as you were physically. My father, for all his effort and sacrifices, lacked that deeper connection. I can count on one hand the number of times I remember hugging him. My first memory of hugging my father, when he came back to Ghana after being away for many years, was a tender moment when I could see his vulnerability. He held me tightly, and I felt the weight of years of longing in that embrace. It wasn't just the physical act of hugging—it was a silent acknowledgment of all the years he had spent away from his family, of all the sacrifices that had piled up on him. I knew that, for him, expressing that kind of affection didn't come easily, but at that moment, he let his guard down. It was a moment I would cherish forever; one I held onto when everything else felt uncertain.

CHAPTER 13
Let the Hunger Games Begin

My stepmother eventually got what she had fought for—her full paycheck—but by then, it didn't matter. The joy had drained from her. She stopped cooking for us every day, and slowly, the cupboards ran empty. As much as I disagreed with my father taking her entire paycheck and leaving her only $20, at least there had been structure. He gave her money for groceries, and there was always food on the table. When my stepmother was allowed by my father to keep her entire paycheck, although she had her own money, neither of them seemed willing to contribute to anything other than the household bills. They held onto their earnings tightly, which meant no food, no new clothes, and no extracurricular activities. The house became a battlefield of silent standoffs with no one willing to budge. My stepmother was a shadow of her former self, and my father's promise of a better life in America began to unravel before our eyes.

When school was in session, we got two meals a day at school, but summers were brutal. There were days we didn't know if we'd eat at all. We'd open the fridge hundreds of times, hoping food would magically appear. We soon realized we had two choices: sit at home and starve or sneak out while our parents were at work to find food wherever we could. As long as we were home before they got back, we figured we'd be fine. When my father would call to speak to one of us and that sibling was not there, the other siblings would cover for them. "They're in the bathroom," we would lie—and my father rarely called back.

Most of our dinners during the school year came from friends' houses. My brother Daniel used to say, "I am going to choose my friends based on how well they feed me when I visit."

It was embarrassing, but it was how we survived. We had to push ourselves out of our comfort zone. Many of the kids in our apartment complex were in the same situation, so we couldn't rely on them for food every night. Eventually, we had to make friends outside of our neighborhood—Which meant white friends who lived in better circumstances.

Most of my meals came from my buddy Simon Flowers' house. We'd do our homework together, and play basketball, and when it was time for dinner, I'd hide in his room, too shy to go out. Simon understood what was happening, so he'd bring me a plate. After a couple of months, his parents caught on. One night, his mom came into the room and said, "Dinner's ready, Kwasi, but you'll have to get your own plate." I was so nervous, so ashamed, but I knew this was the only way to eat. With anxiety surging through me, I'd grab just a little food and rush back to his room.

No matter how many times I went, it never got easier. I never felt comfortable. But Simon, even at a young age, understood kindness. His parents raised him right. In the summer, I practically lived at his house. I'd have all three meals there. Sometimes, when his parents gave him $5 for lunch, he'd meet up with friends at Subway. While the others got footlongs for themselves, Simon would split his with me, giving me half of his sandwich.

The Flowers family taught me trust and showed me that there were good people in the world. I remember the day Simon's dad came home early from work. He sat his family down and explained that his job was cutting his hours. Without hesitation, Simon's mom said, "I'll get a job." It was a beautiful moment of solidarity and support.

After the conversation, Simon's dad came into the room where I was with two other friends. He sat us down and, with clear hurt in his eyes, explained that he couldn't afford to feed us anymore. Seeing the pain on that man's face let me know how much he cared. When everyone left, Simon told me that I wasn't included in that conversation. But out of respect, I started skipping a few nights to ease the burden of being there every day.

Those years were tough, but the kindness of the Flowers family helped me believe that even in the hardest times, there are people who truly care.

CHAPTER 14
Love is Color Blind

S occer wasn't just a game for me—it was the first thing I ever truly fell in love with. My uncle Allan used to practice with the Ghana national team, and whenever he could, he'd bring me along to watch him train. Even as a little kid, I'd run around the sidelines, trying to get the ball from the experienced players while they laughed and showed me a few of their cool tricks. They never passed me the ball, but that didn't matter. Just being there, soaking in their skill and energy, made me feel invincible, and when I played with kids my own age, I was unstoppable. I'd show off the moves those older players had taught me, and the other kids would stop the game, wide-eyed, begging me to teach them. It felt like magic.

In Ghana, playing the game of soccer was pure joy, but in America, it became my lifeline. After we moved across the Atlantic, everything felt strange and unfamiliar, but on the soccer field, I was home. There, I wasn't just another immigrant kid trying to fit in. I was *Kwasi*, the kid with skills that left everyone in awe. Soccer gave me an identity when everything else in my life felt uprooted. Word spread quickly at school about this African kid who was *really* good at soccer. Suddenly, I wasn't invisible anymore, and I felt like I belonged. Soccer gave me the chance to make friends, even beyond our neighborhood--that's when I met Dylan.

When I met Dylan for the first time since leaving Ghana, I felt like I was part of something again. He introduced me to his family, and although they were not rich, they had a big heart and treated me as one of their own. They picked me up for soccer games, making sure I was on the field no matter what. When the team fees were due, Dylan's dad would smooth things over and make sure I was given a scholarship. I was blessed to be such a good soccer player, but I was even more blessed to have Dylan's dad in my life. When he dropped me off after every game, he wouldn't leave until he saw me walk into my apartment building safely. That kind of care, that kind of love, reminded me of the warmth I felt back in Ghana, surrounded by family. Dylan's parents made sure I had breakfast and lunch every Saturday when we spent the day together, and they even pushed me out of my comfort zone, making me order for myself at restaurants. "I'll just have what Dylan's having," I would often say. I didn't want to be a burden.

Through my friendship with Dylan, I learned that family wasn't just about blood—it was about the people who showed up for you, and who cared for you when the world felt heavy. Soccer was my therapy, but Dylan's family gave me a sense of belonging in a world where I often felt lost.

One Saturday, our team had three soccer games scheduled. Between matches, we decided to grab a bite together. While waiting in line at the restaurant, I overheard hushed questions: "Why are Dylan's parents paying for Kwasi? Why don't we ever see his parents?" In that moment, the embarrassment was more than a fleeting feeling—it was a deep, painful awareness of being judged. Every hushed whisper and subtle glance felt like a critique of my family's differences. My stomach churned with anxiety and shame, and I felt exposed as if my personal life were on display. I longed to defend myself but instead shrank into silence, feeling isolated and profoundly vulnerable.

The next day, after two more games, we went out to eat, and I could feel eyes on me even before reaching the restaurant. Not wanting to be the topic of conversation again, I quickly said, "I'm not hungry," when Dylan's dad asked if I wanted something. But he saw the silent storm within me. "You need to eat," he said, pushing a plate toward me. That was just who they were—kind, loving, and protective. Even when I couldn't ask for help, they offered it freely.

Through Dylan's family, I met the Bakers—whose son Arlo was Dylan's best friend. Before long, they embraced me with the same warmth Dylan's family had shown. It felt as though angels had entered my life, offering protection when I needed it most. They provided more than food or rides to games; they gave me a sense of love and belonging I feared was lost when I left Ghana. At home, my father and stepmother had always warned us, "Don't trust white people; they don't like Black people." I understood their caution, shaped by their own experiences—especially after what happened to my brother Kenny.

One night, Kenny and his friend met up with two white girls they knew. The girls' parents were home when they arrived but soon left for dinner, leaving the group alone. Eager to impress, the girls snuck into their dad's liquor cabinet and grabbed a bottle of vodka. They all started drinking, and the girls—trying to keep pace—ended up far too intoxicated. An hour later, they were passed out. Sensing the escalating situation, Kenny's friend left immediately, but Kenny stayed, waiting for the parents to return.

When the father arrived and found his daughters unconscious, he flew into a rage, immediately accusing Kenny of getting them drunk—and worse, of raping them. He called the cops, and both Kenny and his friend were arrested. Under pressure, the girls' father urged his daughters to lie, but by some grace, they chose to tell the truth. They demanded a rape test, and when the results came back negative, authorities cleared both boys of all charges. It was a narrow escape—too close for comfort.

Then I understood why my parents were so wary, but I also saw that not everyone fit that mold. Dylan's and Arlo's families had shown me a different side of the world—a world where love and kindness transcended color.

CHAPTER 15
Soccer—A School
of Hard Knocks

On the field, I was unbeatable. I felt like the best player there, but after my father hit my stepmother, everything changed. My father, who had never attended my games, sat alone in the living room, TV off, and lost in thought. On an impulse, I walked over and asked if he wanted to watch me play. He looked up, puzzled, "Why would I do that?" Without saying a word, I lowered my gaze, grabbed my gear, and left for the game. The disappointment I felt was overwhelming. I had yearned for his presence, hoping that on that day, after everything that had happened, he might show up—not just to watch me play, but to bridge the growing gap between us. Instead, his detached question cut deep, as if my invitation was a burden rather than a plea for connection. I had imagined that my success on the field might finally be something he could take pride in, a chance to step out of his isolation and share in my triumphs. Instead, his response reinforced a painful reality: he had always been distant, more a silent observer than a supportive father. The realization left me feeling abandoned and profoundly disappointed.

That afternoon, from the moment I stepped onto the field, everything shifted. In that game, I discovered a hidden power—a zone where time seemed to slow down, and the entire field moved at my command. By halftime, I had scored four goals and assisted on three more. My coach pulled me from the game, half-joking that I might embarrass the other team even further. I was stunned by what I had just accomplished. It was as if all my pent-up anger and frustration had transformed into unstoppable energy, propelling me to play better than ever before. I couldn't wait to experience that surge again, and sure enough, the next game delivered the same extraordinary results.

I discovered a way to channel my rage that felt incredible—but I soon learned that anger is a beast, dangerous and unpredictable. A single poke or small insult could flip me from focused to furious, ready to fight. Managing it became a constant challenge. In some games, I'd score three or four goals: in others, I'd be benched for losing control. Opposing teams noticed, and so did my own team. Not everyone embraced me like Dylan's family did—some teammates even envied the spotlight I carried. I was the star, a beacon they wanted for themselves.

By the time I hit seventh and eighth grade, I was playing high school soccer. That round ball I used to kick around in Ghana with my dirty bare feet had begun to change my life. Suddenly, Kwasi was a name people knew—popular at school, featured in the local newspaper, and even appearing on TV. My father started to hear about me when his friends brought him clippings from the newspaper—I found those clippings in his room. Once, I caught him watching one of my games on TV. As soon as I walked in, he quickly changed the channel, pretending he wasn't paying attention. It was a great feeling, but it came with a weight.

As the best player on the team, especially as an eighth grader, the pressure was immense. I was the star, but our team wasn't great. We lost more games than we won, and when we lost, the blame fell squarely on my shoulders. I remember one game in particular when we were facing our biggest rival, the Hill. Before the match, the seniors on the team and our captain came to me. "Kwasi, we need you today. We've never beaten the Hill. You have to make it happen for us." I'd never felt pressure like that before, but I wanted to deliver for them.

The rain poured down in sheets, turning the field into a slick, slippery mess. Mud clung to our cleats, every step a struggle to maintain balance. It was a tie game at 2-2. Then, the ball came to me. My heart thundered in my chest as I trapped it with my foot. It felt like I was fighting against the elements, the wet surface making each movement feel uncertain. I glanced up and saw two defenders closing in, their eyes locked on me. Without thinking, I faked to the left and slipped past them, leaving them to tumble helplessly into the mud. It was just me and the goal, and with the shouts of my teammates ringing in my ears, all I could focus on was the net ahead of me. With their voices a distant encouragement, my pulse was a drumbeat, loud in my head, as I drew my leg back and prepared to strike.

I kicked with everything I had, the mud flying from my foot as the ball left it. The ball veered off to the side, spinning wide and out of bounds. I watched it sail away, my heart sinking with it. The referee's whistle cut through the silence, signaling the end of the game. I dropped to my knees in the mud, the cold rain soaking through my clothes, mingling with the bitter mix of frustration and guilt that weighed down on me. My breath came in ragged gasps as I stared at the empty goal, the realization sinking in that I had failed again.

A painful memory surged in my mind. I'd been there before—in the rain, missing a crucial shot, and as a consequence, I lost my best friend, Yaw. His face, laughter, and voice flickered through my mind like ghosts from the past. I could feel history repeating itself, and a paralyzing fear gripped me as if I were about to lose something far more precious than the game itself. My teammates passed by me in silence, their footsteps fading into the distance, leaving me isolated. The weight of rejection and the looming threat of loss pressed down on me, intensifying my despair as the captain looked at me and said, "We don't need you anyway."

Soon after, during practice, we were in a circle doing jumping jacks when I had an itch on my leg. I stopped for just a second to scratch it, and out of nowhere, all three captains started screaming at me, tearing me down for something as small as scratching my leg. I couldn't believe it. I was frustrated, confused, and trapped. Soccer was my escape—the one place where I felt like I belonged, but I felt my sanctuary crumbling. My home life was already a mess, and the only thing that made sense to me was becoming just another source of pain.

I felt the pressure mounting, but I kept my composure, walked away, and sat on the sidelines, sipping water to steady myself. One of my teammates—someone who rarely spoke up—approached me. He was visibly anxious when he confided, "Bro, they've been holding secret meetings to push you over the edge so they can kick you off the team. Even Coach Ron warned that you only have one chance—if you snap, you're out." That revelation was a turning point. It became painfully clear they no longer wanted me around and were waiting for me to crack. From that moment, I withdrew, stopped putting forth any effort, and faded into the background. I simply showed up and went through the motions.

The day before our first game, practice was brutal. At the end of practice, Coach Ron instructed the team to run five miles. No one was happy about it, but we all started running anyway—everyone except Jefferson. Jefferson was another star player that teammates and coaches frequently compared me to. He was just standing there, watching. We were halfway through the run, and my emotions building with every step until I couldn't take it anymore. I was tired of him getting treated differently, so I stopped running. I grabbed my water and sat down. It wasn't even two seconds before I saw all three captains sprinting toward me, screaming at the top of their lungs, "Kwasi, why aren't you running?!" One of them grabbed my hand, trying to pull me up. I yanked my hand away, and asked, "Why isn't Jefferson running? Why haven't you gone up to him and yelled at him?" I lost it. I just couldn't take it anymore. Most of the time, when I reach my breaking point, it has nothing to do with the game. It's usually something that happened at home, something weighing on me. But this time was different. This time, I was selfish with my emotions. It felt like they were trying to take away the one thing I truly loved. The team erupted in a frenzy, yelling at me like a pack of wolves. When Coach Ron noticed the chaos, he approached me, and without asking what was happening, he looked straight at me and said, "Kwasi, you're off the team!" I was stunned. "I'm just a Black man trying to play soccer." I emphatically replied. My words, intended to express my sense of injustice, were misinterpreted by

Coach Ron as an accusation of racism. Those words cost me dearly, affecting me for the rest of my high school years.

Coach Ron, who was also a teacher at school, spread the word among the faculty that I had called him racist. After that, it seemed like every teacher had it out for me. Suddenly, I was no longer just a soccer player—I was the "bad kid from Southside," marked by a label that followed me everywhere I went. It was one of the darkest times in my life. To them, soccer was just a game, but to me, it was my escape, my therapy, and it gave me a sense of belonging.

I stood before my teammates, poured my heart out in a passionate plea, and asked for another chance to play. After my speech, they asked me to step outside so they could vote. I waited outside until the vote was over. One by one, my teammates; guys who I had played soccer with since I was ten, walked out of the room, their heads down, avoiding my gaze. These were the same friends I had grown up with on the field, yet that day, not one of them could look me in the eye. Finally, Coach Ron approached and said, "They voted. You're off the team." I was devastated.

I later learned that only three out of twenty-five teammates had voted for me to stay. Seeing them every day—in classes, even gym— was unbearable. They still couldn't make eye contact with me, ashamed of what had happened. One even said, "Sorry, I voted for you." But when others claimed the same, I realized something was off: I had three votes, yet four claimed they supported me. It felt like a knife was twisting in my gut. It all felt like a cruel joke.

That season, winning the state championship was expected to hinge on both Jefferson and me playing. With me sidelined because

I was voted off the team, the plan unraveled. Sitting at the back and watching the game, I could feel the judgment in every parent's stare. Labeled the "bad kid," I struggled with the weight of everyone else's definition of me. But even as those doubts crept in, I kept repeating, "If you never fell, then you never climbed," reminding myself that setbacks were simply part of the climb.

During the playoffs, I wanted to go to the game, but I didn't have a ride. I was about to walk home when Jefferson's dad saw me. He asked if I was going, and when I told him I didn't have a way to get there, he simply said, "Get in." I was shocked—he didn't look at me with those judging eyes. He didn't care about the rumors. Instead, we talked about life, about everything except soccer. He gave me advice, real advice that I'll never forget. By the time he dropped me off at home, he looked at me and said, "Kwasi, you are not who they say you are. I'm glad you chose to ride with me." I wanted to break down and cry, but I held it together. I apologized, and he asked, "For what?" I told him, "Sometimes it feels like they're trying to pit me and Jefferson against each other. I can't stand it when they say your son is better than me. I'm a competitor." He smiled and gave me one of the best pieces of advice I've ever received: "Have you noticed they never say that they, themselves, are better than you?"

That conversation changed everything. I finally understood why everyone loved Jefferson. It all started at home—with the way his family treated people. The next season, I met his mom, and she was just as kind as his dad. I realized how blind I had been, consumed with trying to prove I was better than him instead of working together with him. I learned a valuable lesson—not everyone you fight is your enemy and not everyone that helps you is your friend. Comparison is a thief of joy, so I learned to live life at my own pace.

That next season, Jefferson and I united, watching each other's backs. No one dared mess with me because he was always there and wouldn't let them. The result was magical. We clinched our school's first-ever state soccer championship!

CHAPTER 16
Fresh Love: New Passion

In my senior year of high school, soccer was still my first love. My brother, Kenny, had just started dating a girl from school who was from Ghana. When she wanted Kenny to meet her mom, he nervously asked me to join him. He wanted to make his best impression, so I agreed to go with him, just to give him a level of comfort. We arrived at her house, and as soon as her mom opened the door, time seemed to freeze. She was stunning! Kenny and I exchanged surprised glances, both of us caught off guard by her beauty. Later, we joked with his girlfriend about how gorgeous her mom was. Although she laughed it off, she must have mentioned it because soon after, we received an invitation to dinner and a movie at their place.

At dinner, I noticed her mom acting flirtatiously, but Kenny and I just shrugged it off. As the invitations kept coming, I thought Kenny was comfortable enough to go without me. I didn't want to intrude, so eventually I skipped out on one of the invitations. The next day at school, his girlfriend approached and said, "My mom's mad at you."

"What did I do?" I wondered. She explained that because of my absence, her mother felt slighted. I was perplexed by that, but I wanted to smooth things over, so I asked her to call her mom so that

I could apologize. On the phone, she flirted even more, offering me her number "if I ever needed anything." Later that night, Kenny came into my room grinning from ear to ear. "Bro! I think her mom really likes you!" I joked and asked him to pass my number along to her, and a few minutes later, my phone rang—it was her. The calls became a thrilling nightly ritual; the attention from such a beautiful, mature woman in her forties was undeniably exciting. I wasn't your normal teenager; I was a teenager with his own mommy issues.

When I told my friends about it, they didn't believe me until they started seeing her picking me and Kenny up from school in her Lexus. Our conversations continued for months. When Valentine's Day came around, I wanted to do something special for her, so I scraped together enough money for some flowers and chocolates from the dollar store. When I handed her the gift, she was more thrilled than I expected. The next day, she surprised me with a much fancier box of chocolates and a card, asking me not to open it until I got home. Later that night, I opened the envelope to read the card and found $300 inside. My heart tightened. I had never received that kind of generosity before; it felt like someone truly cared for me. That night, during our call, I opened up about my life and fears. She asked why I hadn't kissed her yet and then said, "Don't be afraid." Her words stirred a disturbing childhood memory from my time in Ghana.

When I was about seven, after my grandmother passed away, my busy mother—often on the road for her fish market—hired a babysitter. One night, while I was asleep, I was gently shaken awake. Groggy and confused, I opened my eyes to find the babysitter looming over me. Before I could make sense of what was happening, she began doing things to me that no child should ever have to endure. I froze, paralyzed with fear and confusion, unable to comprehend what was happening or why. She looked me right in the eyes, fully aware of my terror, and whispered, "Don't be afraid." Her words felt hollow and cruel, fear had already overtaken me. Night after night, it continued.

The house was quiet, the air heavy with silence, and I was trapped in a nightmare I couldn't escape. I didn't tell anyone—not even my mother, because I didn't have the words. How could I explain to someone something I didn't fully understand myself? A part of me thought no one would believe me and another part feared the consequences if they did. Eventually, the babysitter was fired for reasons unrelated to what she had done to me. The nightmare stopped, but the damage was done. As I grew older, I tried to bury the memories, but they haunted me. By the time I hit my teenage years, I had found a way to cope with humor. I joked about it sometimes, turning my pain into punchlines, pretending it didn't matter. In our community, what happened to me wasn't seen as abuse—it was treated as a kind of twisted badge of honor. For a boy, especially a young one, being noticed by an older woman was celebrated. It was considered bragging rights, so to admit that I felt violated, scared, or ashamed would have gone against everything our culture said I should feel. Boys were expected to puff their chests and smile at the idea of an experience like that, but the truth was far from the bravado. Behind the jokes and the forced smile was a scared little boy who didn't feel proud or accomplished—just confused and deeply ashamed.

I carried that shame with me for years, hiding it behind the laughter and the cultural expectations that told me I should have felt lucky. I knew there was nothing lucky about what happened to me. I still grapple with the weight of those memories. It wasn't just that it happened—it was the silence, the isolation, and the way my pain was dismissed by a culture that refused to see boys as victims. It's a burden I'm still learning how to release. Those words, "Don't be afraid," triggered those memories, and I found myself, once again, caught in another complicated situation.

CHAPTER 17
Breaking up is Hard to Do

I was in a relationship with a woman who provided me with everything—clothes, food, and even a laptop for college. She was like a sugar momma, and my brothers also benefited from her generosity. For the first time, I felt like someone genuinely wanted to take care of me. However, over time, I noticed a shift in our relationship. The line between care and control, between affection and harm, became increasingly blurred, and I couldn't tell where one ended and the other began. It started as something subtle, but before long it was impossible to ignore. She started to take over aspects of my life that I was perfectly capable of handling. I told myself it was her way of supporting me during a tough time, but deep down, I wasn't happy about it. I felt it went beyond caring about me or helping me; it was about taking my independence.

I've always worked hard for everything I have. Even as a boy, I took pride in my hard work, knowing that my accomplishments came from my own sweat and grit. That work ethic was a fundamental part of who I was, but over time, I felt it slipping away. It wasn't that she meant harm—I knew her intentions were kind—but my independence was a part of my identity, and I wasn't willing to let her take that from me. It wasn't a decision made lightly, but I felt it was necessary to break up with her.

I often wondered if what we had was truly love. She cared for me deeply, and in many ways, I appreciated her care more than I could express. I was at a point in my life when I needed a steady presence to help me navigate the chaos I was experiencing, and in that sense, I often thought of her as a blessing. I saw her as someone God had sent to me during a season when I didn't even realize how much I needed help.

Reflecting on those times, I can see that our time together was a gift, even if it didn't last. It taught me a lot about myself—about what I need, what I value, and what I'm willing to compromise for the sake of a relationship. Life is a collection of experiences, each one shaping us in ways we can't always see in the moment. I saw that relationship as one that challenged me, comforted me, and ultimately taught me lessons that I still apply to my life. Sharing this story from a position of gratitude for the growth it brought me, I learned that not every chapter in life is meant to last forever. Some chapters are simply guides to the next. I carried the lessons from that relationship—the value of care, the importance of independence, and the need for balance—into my next chance at love. I approached love with a deeper understanding of who I was and what I needed, refusing to compromise the parts of myself that defined me.

When love came around again, I was ready to embrace it fully, but on my own terms. I wanted a partnership, not a dynamic where one person carried the other. I wanted to share my life with someone, not lose myself in them, and when that chance finally came, I leaned into it with a clarity and confidence I hadn't had before. That experience wasn't just a lesson; it was preparation. It taught me what to hold on to, what to let go of, and how to build something stronger the second time around.

CHAPTER 18
Could This Be Love?

I t was a beautiful Saturday afternoon, one of those days when everything just felt perfect. The sun was shining, a gentle breeze carried the promise of a good time, and I had been invited to a friend's birthday party. Something about the day made me want to step things up a notch. I decided I'd show up in style, making an unforgettable impression. I pulled out my best outfit—the one I thought screamed confidence and charisma. I was convinced I was about to turn heads.

When I arrived at the party, I mustered all the confidence I could. Scanning the crowd, my eyes landed on her—a girl I'd seen around town but never had the courage to approach. She was stunning, a beauty that left me momentarily breathless. My heart quickened, yet I tried to play it cool. Lacking a healthy attachment to the word "lucky," I wondered if it was divine intervention that placed me at a table right next to her.

I was so nervous I could barely think, and I think she sensed it. My eyes kept drifting toward her until she finally caught me staring. She smiled warmly, leaned in slightly, and said, "I love your outfit." I froze for a moment—my carefully chosen outfit was the focus of her attention? Her compliment instantly boosted my confidence. I thanked her a bit awkwardly at first, and as we introduced ourselves, she smiled and said, "I'm Scarlett."

We flirted all night, trading smiles, teasing comments, and a playful energy that made the room around us vanish. For those few hours, it felt like just the two of us. As the party wound down, my nerves returned. I didn't want the connection to end, yet I was too shy to ask for her number directly. Instead, I casually mentioned, "I might head to a local bar tonight," hoping she'd suggest joining me. She offered no response—no reaction, no acknowledgment. Convinced she wasn't interested, I let it go. We said our goodbyes, and once I reached my car, I couldn't help but kick myself. I replayed the evening, analyzing every word and moment. Although I hadn't secured her number, I cherished the memory of making an impression and sharing a connection with someone who once seemed out of reach. It was a reminder that sometimes you have to just take the leap. Next time, I vowed, I won't let the moment pass me by.

A month later, my friends convinced me to step out with them for a night at the same bar I mentioned to Scarlett a month earlier. As soon as we entered, someone grabbed my arm. I turned around, and to my astonishment, it was her. "Are you just going to walk by me?" she teased, a smile lighting up her face. She later admitted she had come to the bar on the night we first met and was crushed that I never showed up. She also confessed that she had been coming to that bar every Saturday since, hoping to catch a glimpse of me. My heart soared, and without hesitation, I asked for her number. We talked and danced the night away, the chemistry between us was electric. Could this be the love I had always longed for?

I knew Scarlett would be my wife right away, but the fear of commitment had me questioning everything. It didn't help that she moved into my apartment the second night after we met at the bar. I had never lived with a girlfriend before, and things were moving too fast for my liking. My insecurities wouldn't allow me to let her pay any bills—if things didn't work out, I wanted the option to ask her to leave without any complications. I was already planning for the worst instead of letting down my guard and trusting her.

I kept a safe distance, afraid of surrendering completely to the love she was offering. It wasn't that I didn't care—if anything, I cared too much. The weight of my past, my insecurities, and the fear of losing myself in something so deep made me hesitant.

At first, Scarlett was patient. She met my resistance with understanding, giving me space when I pulled away and reassuring me when I struggled to find the words to explain myself. But over time, the warmth between us began to cool. Where there was once laughter and effortless conversation, tension crept in. Small misunderstandings turned into long silences and silence into arguments.

She wanted certainty; I gave her hesitation. She needed reassurance; I offered half-hearted promises. I could see the hurt in her eyes every time she reached for me and found me holding back. Eventually, my fear turned into suspicion. I started questioning her every move, doubting her loyalty when she went out with friends, convincing myself that she was slipping away. But it wasn't her actions that were the problem—it was my own insecurity. Scarlett had reached her breaking point.

"I can't do this anymore," she said, standing in the doorway, her voice steady but laced with finality. "I won't keep fighting for someone who won't fight for me." And just like that, she was gone.

My heart shattered as I watched her walk away, realizing too late that the love I had feared losing was slipping through my fingers. That night, something in me shifted. I knew the only way our relationship could work was if I fully trusted her. No more hesitation. No more fear. I was scared, but I wasn't willing to lose her. I swallowed my pride and begged her to give us another chance. I asked her to be patient with me, to be gentle with my heart, and with all the love she had left, she did just that.

Scarlett treated my heart with tenderness, loving me in ways that were both new and deeply healing. Slowly but surely, the "Great Wall of China" I had built around myself out of fear crumbled. Trust was something I had never given fully to anyone, yet with Scarlett, I found myself letting go, surrendering my heart to her without hesitation. They say that when you know, you know—and with Scarlett, it felt as though I had known her forever. We have now been together for nine years and married for four. Our journey has been far from perfect, but it has been real—filled with love, growth, and lessons that have shaped us into the couple we are today. All relationships face challenges, but we've learned how to navigate them together. Where we once let fear and miscommunication create distance, we now lean on trust and honesty to bridge the gaps.

We've come to understand that love isn't about never struggling—it's about choosing each other even when things get hard. We listen more, assume less, and make space for each other's needs. We've learned that patience, grace, and vulnerability aren't weaknesses but the foundation of a strong marriage.

Looking back, I realize that the best decision I ever made wasn't just fighting for our relationship—it was learning how to show up for Scarlett in the way she deserved. The result? Every day, I continue choosing her, just as she continues choosing me.

CHAPTER 19
Reconnecting With my First Love

I was just starting college, and it had been eight long years since I last spoke to my mother—eight years without a word, letter, or any sign that she still cared or remembered us. I often wondered if she ever thought about me or how I was doing. As painful as those thoughts were, I reminded myself that some things are beyond my control, and I had no choice but to keep moving forward.

It had been months since my father had checked in, so when he finally called, it felt unexpected. He didn't call just to chat; his tone hinted at something more. My thoughts had long been occupied with my mother, though I had hesitated to mention her. Summoning every ounce of courage, I finally asked about her.

"She's doing well," my father replied calmly, then, without missing a beat, he asked, "Would you like her number?"

My chest tightened as a surge of emotions washed over me. Eight years of silence and endless wondering suddenly gave way to the possibility of reconnecting—a door, once firmly closed, was cracked open. While my father's steady voice provided a semblance of reassurance, my voice trembled as I stammered, "Yes, I would."

"You're eighteen now," he continued. "It's time you two talked."

Tears streamed down my face as I shakily scribbled her number on a scrap of paper. For years, I'd convinced myself I didn't need to hear from her, but now I realized how wrong I'd been—something long buried was finally ready to speak. For days, I stared at that paper, paralyzed by fear. What could I possibly say after all this time? What if she didn't want to hear from me? I made excuse after excuse, promising myself I'd call later. Then, a week later, my phone buzzed with an unfamiliar number—not a U.S. number. I hesitated, but after a few rings, I finally answered.

"Paa Kwasi, Paa Kwasi, is this you?"

My mother's voice broke through the line, shaky and unmistakably hers. For a moment, I couldn't find my words, every emotion I'd buried over the years was bubbling to the surface. I managed to hold it together, and we talked for over an hour. The sound of her voice filled a void I hadn't even realized had grown so large. It felt like a piece of myself I'd lost had suddenly been put back in place.

As the conversation came to an end, she asked,

"Can you send me some money, my son?"

Her voice was soft, almost apologetic, but her words hit me hard. I was just a broke college kid, barely scraping by on odd jobs and campus work.

"Of course, Mom," I said, without hesitation.

After all those years away from her, I wanted so badly to do something for her, so I hustled like never before, taking on extra work wherever I could. I sent her $100. Her gratitude was overwhelming, and I felt good to finally be able to give back to her. My mother's sacrifice was the heartbreaking decision she made to allow us to come to America while she stayed behind. It took courage for her to watch us leave, knowing it would be years before she saw us again. I felt like I owed her for that.

Our conversations became a weekly ritual, and I cherished each one of them. Each time, she would ask about my life and my studies, and invariably, she requested money. Initially, I didn't mind, but over time, her requests grew heavier, more frequent. What once felt like a gesture of love started to feel more like an obligation. One day, I mustered the courage to ask her...

"Is everything okay?"

She hesitated before answering in a voice quieter than usual.

"Your father hasn't been helping me. I have nothing left," she confided.

Her words cut deep. I wanted to help, but I was struggling myself—torn between honoring the sacrifices made for me and grappling with my own limitations. Reconnecting with my mother, my first love, was bittersweet; every dollar I sent reminded me how complicated love could be. As beautiful as love was, it was also a burden. I realized then that the weight of love had been with me for a long time—the first true taste of it being when my older brother Kyle left home to attend college.

That moment marked the beginning of understanding that love, no matter how cherished, often comes with heavy responsibilities. It was a lesson I would carry into the next chapter of my life.

CHAPTER 20
The Burden of Love

When I was in the eighth grade, Kyle, who had been the steady foundation in our household, left for college. He was the first one to leave without any conflict or drama, and I admired him for that. I watched how my other siblings left the house—full of tension, unresolved issues, and chaos—I didn't want that for myself. Kyle was different. He seemed to have it all figured out, so I watched closely.

He worked at KFC and always brought home food to share. He handed down his clothes to me, which I handed down to Daniel, and Daniel gave his to Kenny. Poor Kenny. By the time those clothes made their way to him, they were so worn out they were barely worth wearing.

Kyle's departure left a gap, a silence in the house that I wasn't sure how to fill. I realized then how much his presence had kept things together, and with him gone, everything felt uncertain. Suddenly, at 14, I was the man of the house, and I didn't have the slightest idea how I was going to take care of my little brothers. Our parents were so wrapped up in their own problems they didn't even know where we were or what we were doing most of the time. My father stopped checking on us, and he didn't care about our grades like he used to. I had to set a standard for myself and my brothers, and they followed. Deep down, they knew I was the only one looking out for them.

I got a job at KFC, just like Kyle had, but I didn't tell my father. I knew if he found out, he'd take my whole paycheck like he had done to my other siblings. I worked hard that summer, saving every dollar I could so we'd have school clothes and supplies. When tax season came, I'd grab the mail before my father saw it, and tossed out my W-2 forms, because if he knew, it wouldn't end well for me. After Kyle left for college, he no longer had the burden of caring for us, so when I headed off to college, I thought my burden would also end, until my father announced he was moving back to Ghana.

The news hit me like a bomb when he said his move would be permanent.

"What about my little brothers?" I asked, panic rising in my chest.

"They'll stay with your brother, Kevin," he said, like it was nothing.

I couldn't believe it. Kevin was already living in a cramped three-bedroom apartment with his wife and three kids. There was no space for my brothers. I immediately called Kevin, and he confirmed—there was absolutely no room. Furious, I called my father back, but he brushed me off. I was filled with disappointment and anger. *How could he just abandon his children like that?* My brothers called me daily, their voices laced with worry. I was miles away at school, but the burden of being the man of the house was thrust back on me. My father was set to leave in six months, but I kept reassuring them that we would figure it out together. I reminded them that we'd come to America together and always had each other's backs.

Each day, they called to share stories, proudly updating me on their latest feats in soccer. They were determined to surpass my freshman record of twenty-four goals in a season, and their enthusiasm gave me strength. They didn't know it, but the way they looked up to me kept me going.

As the countdown to my father's departure to Ghana ticked down to three months, I returned home for summer break. I took on two jobs. My night shift ran from 7 p.m. to 7 a.m., then I clocked in for my second job from 9 a.m. to 3 p.m. I barely had time to sleep, and although it was an unsustainable schedule, I pushed through. By the end of the summer, I had saved enough money to secure an apartment for me and my two teenaged brothers. When the day came for my father to leave, my brothers and I helped him pack.

As he was preparing to leave for Ghana, he was oblivious to the fact that we had secured our own place to live. He didn't ask; he didn't care.

He left us—not a single hug, no goodbyes—nothing.

"Just go to Kevin's place," he demanded, as he walked out the door.

I lost all respect for him that day. He abandoned us, like it was nothing, and that was the last time we saw him.

At 20, I was suddenly a father figure, and it felt like the blind leading the blind because I was barely more than a kid myself. I transferred to a local college, both of my brothers got jobs, and we all agreed to do whatever it took to keep that roof over our heads. Between keeping up with school, looking after my brothers, and my mother calling me monthly for money, life became a hustle. None of my older siblings stepped up to help, and bitterness simmered within me. My heart became hardened by my disappointment, especially toward Kevin. He'd convinced our father he'd take us in, knowing all along that wasn't true. The weight of everything, the disappointments and letdowns, hardened me. If it weren't for my little brothers and my mother, who I'd never stop caring for, I didn't have room in my heart for much else.

Not long after that, I stood in Kevin's room in the intensive care unit of the hospital. Surrounded by the hum of machines and the quiet sobs of others, I felt nothing. When he passed, a cold and hollow void replaced the sadness I should have felt. Instead, I looked at my brother and I prayed. I did not pray for comfort; I prayed for clarity and the strength to release my anger. I didn't hate him, but I couldn't fix what was unresolved between us. Numbing my pain became my coping mechanism, and even in prayer, I wasn't sure I was ready to let go of that numbness—it felt like it was the only thing holding me together.

As the months passed, my younger brothers and I scraped by on what little we had. After rent and bills, there was barely enough left for food. But this struggle was nothing new—it was a familiar rhythm we had learned to accept. Some days, the fridge was more empty than full, and we often shared what little we had. We turned survival into an art, finding comfort even in splitting the last bit of change for a simple treat like pizza. There was a quiet strength in our shared struggle; the bond between us became the foundation of our resilience, giving us the power to push through, no matter what.

CHAPTER 21
Going Back to Ghana

My junior year of college was in full swing when I decided to visit my old campus and reconnect with my former roommate, Paul. We hadn't seen each other in years, and when we reconnected, his usual spark was missing. Something was weighing on him. I didn't know how to bring it up, but later that night, Paul broke down. Between choked sobs, he told me that his dad had passed away, and he'd been struggling with his passing ever since. His father was his hero, and after his parents' divorce, he chose to stay with him because he looked up to him in every way. The news hit me harder than I expected. In the short time I'd known Paul's dad, he'd taught me so much. He didn't see race; he saw character. He didn't care about the color of your skin but only if you were good or bad. That memory of his integrity, now tied to the grief in Paul's voice, shook me deeply. I couldn't help but wonder, *What if I lost my mother?* She was my anchor, my connection to everything we'd left behind in Ghana, and I hadn't seen her in over eleven years. It was time—I knew I had to go back to Ghana, and I convinced my brother Daniel to come along.

Daniel and my mother's relationship had always been complicated. He was eight when we left Ghana, and the years had blurred his memories of our home. Although he understood Twi, our language, he struggled to speak it. Like me, Daniel had spent most of his life in America, so we both knew we were in for a massive cultural shock.

We finally arrived at the airport in Ghana after a long and tiring twenty-four-hour travel day, but we had another long drive before we would have the reunion we'd waited over a decade for. On the fourteen-hour ride to my grandmother's house, I saw a side of Ghana that was both familiar and foreign. I barely remembered the villages, the bustling streets, and the countryside we were rolling by. When we finally arrived, suddenly, all the comforts of America felt distant. I didn't realize how different life was until I saw the conditions we once lived in. I was deeply humbled. When we pulled up to our mother's home, eleven years of distance vanished in an instant. She opened her arms to me and Daniel, her smile wide and her hug warm and fierce. Despite that joy, there was no denying we were strangers. My mother felt like a mystery waiting to be unraveled, but each night, we'd sit together for hours, praying, talking, and catching up. I became the translator between Daniel and our mother, bridging the years of separation with each shared word. Those conversations healed parts of me I didn't even know were broken. For the first time in a long time, I felt like a kid again, free of responsibility and grounded in my family's love.

Our mother had managed to build a stable life for herself, and it was a relief to see her doing well, finally secure in her own right. Each day, Daniel and I helped her with her business, and we soaked in every moment with her. I was puzzled that she didn't bring us around the extended family much. I couldn't understand why, and I didn't press the issue. One day, we decided to visit our old house. As a kid, I thought we were well-off, especially after my father returned that day with a private car and brand-new bicycles for us. But as I stood there, older, I realized just how much our mother had done to make ends meet. She'd shielded us from the harsh realities of life, making everything work despite the odds, and I'd been too young to know any better.

Our short visit back to Ghana was a gift I'd cherish forever. Those weeks with our mother were some of the happiest days of my life. It felt like a homecoming to my own soul, a reminder of where I came from and the strength I carried forward. While there, Daniel and I were also reunited with our full sister, Joy.

In July of 2003, when I was fourteen, my parents welcomed Joy into the world. My mother already had three boys: one from her previous marriage and two with my father. When my father told me about the new baby, my first reaction was worry. My parents were already struggling to care for us, so how could he bring another child into the world?

When my father moved back to Ghana, he left my mother with Joy and never called again. Joy became my mother's responsibility, my father, once again, leaving a trail of broken promises. Eventually, my mother filed for divorce, freeing herself from his abandonment. When it was time for us to return to America, she begged us to take Joy with us. As much as I wanted to say yes, the harsh reality was we were college students struggling to make ends meet, and we simply couldn't afford to care for a 10-year-old girl. As we prepared to leave, Joy clung to me, her tear-streaked face silently pleading to come along. My mother's cries pierced my heart as we said our goodbyes. I held back my tears, vowing not to show my pain in front of her or my siblings. I promised to return after graduation.

CHAPTER 22
The Daniel Story

The trip back to Ghana was a stark reminder of the disparities between life in America and life back home. Our life in America wasn't ideal by any means, but I couldn't shake the thought that we were still better off than many in Ghana. That new perspective became the fuel for my drive. I was determined to make something of my life, not just for myself, but for Joy, Daniel, Kenny, my family, and the countless sacrifices my parents had made. My relentless focus on survival and progress created an unspoken rift between me and my brothers. I saw the bigger picture and the risks that came with it—one wrong decision, one reckless choice, and we could lose everything. My brothers saw things differently. I understood their frustration—they wanted freedom, while I bore the weight of responsibility. I envied their ability to chase small joys while I stayed up at night, calculating bills and worrying about the future. I tried to warn them, reminding them of the precariousness of our situation, but my words often came off as lectures which alienated them from me even further.

One Saturday morning, my younger brother Daniel sat me down, his face a mixture of excitement and anxiety. "I've got some news," he said. "Me and Leah...we're having a baby."

My heart swelled with pride, fear, and a deep sense of concern. Daniel was only 20, barely an adult himself. How could he take care of a baby when he was still figuring out his own life? To my surprise, Daniel stepped up. He and Leah decided to get a small apartment and move in together and he took on a full-time job while juggling school. Watching him hustle and make sacrifices of his own, it became clear to me that, despite the tension between us, the foundation I'd been trying to build for our family had made an impact. He was growing into a man I respected, and his success reaffirmed the purpose behind my sacrifices. Two months later, my niece was born, and I paid them all a visit in their small but cozy apartment, filled with baby gear and the sweet sounds of newborn coos. As I sat down with Daniel to catch up, the unfulfilled promise we made to our mother loomed over us.

"Mom's been asking when we're going to come and get Joy," he said.

Things were finally stabilizing for me. My other brother, Kenny, was preparing for a new venture in Florida, so I suggested to Daniel that he take on the responsibility of bringing Joy over. I had done my part, and it seemed fair to pass the torch, but Daniel's girlfriend shut the idea down almost immediately.

"He's not in a position to take that on," she said firmly, her words cutting through the room. She had seen the toll it took on us to hold our family together. I realized my sacrifices had distanced me from my brothers—Daniel's success reflected the foundation I built, but it also highlighted a painful truth: I had become a leader in our family, but a stranger to my own brothers.

Daniel was my full brother, two years younger than me, but in many ways, he was my best friend. Back in Ghana, we were inseparable. He was the annoying little brother I often wrestled with, but I was fiercely protective of him. I knew Daniel had it toughest when we moved from Ghana to America. When Daniel left Ghana at just eight years old, he was the youngest of my mother's children, facing the harsh reality of a new world alone. I watched as he struggled, especially after our father cut off the phone calls to our mother. And watching our other siblings reunite with their mother definitely didn't make it any easier for Daniel or me. It was a bittersweet reminder of what we had sacrificed and what we had missed. The joy on their faces, the laughter, and the ease with which they embraced her filled the room like sunlight breaking through storm clouds. For them, it was a long-awaited moment of healing, a piece of their hearts finally restored. But for Daniel and me, it was different.

We lost our mother, but she had not died. It's hard to explain what it feels like to grieve for someone who's still alive. The pain was sharp and constant, like a wound that wouldn't heal. She was out there, somewhere, and yet completely out of reach. Not being able to talk to her, to hear her voice, made matters even worse. It was as though she existed only in memories and fragments of stories we clung to like lifelines. When Daniel's ninth birthday rolled around, neither my father nor my stepmother acknowledged it. I could see the sadness in Daniel's eyes, but I didn't know how to lift his spirits. That afternoon, my father came home with Chinese food. While Daniel and I sat in the living room, our father casually took out a single plate for himself and settled at the kitchen table to eat, oblivious to our rumbling stomachs. He devoured the food while we watched, our hunger gnawing at us. After my father hopped in the shower to prepare for his next shift, Daniel and I polished off his uneaten food, leaving the empty container tucked away in the fridge, hoping he wouldn't discover it. When he emerged from the shower, he went straight for the fridge and discovered the empty container. He stormed over to us demanding to know who had eaten his food. We sat there, silent and guilty, the weight of his disappointment heavy in the air.

Weathering the storm of our father's anger, I saw a chance to give Daniel something special on his birthday. I ran to my room, yanked open my drawer, and grabbed my piggy bank. Sitting cross-legged on the floor, I shook it hard, the clinking of coins echoing my desperation. When I finally finished counting, I had $3. Without hesitation, I grabbed Daniel's hand and led him to the nearby Chinese restaurant, the one we always walked by but rarely entered. As we stood at the counter, I looked up at the owner, nervous but determined.

"Sir, I only have $3" I said, holding out the crumpled bills and loose coins. "We're fifteen cents short, but it's my brother's birthday. Can we still get the plate of food?" I asked.

The owner paused, studying us for a moment. I braced myself for a refusal, already preparing to walk away with Daniel, but the owner smiled warmly.

"Don't worry about it," he said, waving his hand dismissively.

Relief washed over me as he handed us the food, treating us like honored guests instead of kids with empty pockets. We found a seat in the corner, and for the first time in what felt like forever, we sat and ate without worrying about the world outside. The noodles, the chicken, the sauce—it tasted like a feast, not because of the food itself, but because of the joy it brought Daniel. He laughed, cracked jokes, and we talked for hours about nothing and everything, savoring each bite and each moment.

As we walked home, the cool evening breeze brushing against our faces, Daniel's happiness was unmistakable. He kept thanking me, saying how it was the best birthday he'd ever had. I always thought about how to protect him from feeling the weight of our circumstances, but it was beginning to feel more like a heavy responsibility. That plate of food wasn't just a meal—it was a symbol of the sacrifices I'd have to make for him, putting his needs before my own. As much as I loved him, that responsibility began to strain our bond.

Daniel and I weren't just two brothers navigating life together anymore. I was the one saying "no" when he wanted to do something reckless, the one reminding him of our reality when he just wanted to forget. I became the one he resented when he wanted freedom and the one he looked to when he needed support.

Our conversation about bringing Joy to America didn't go as I'd hoped. I knew Daniel was overwhelmed, but his rejection of the idea left the weight of responsibility squarely back on my shoulders. That afternoon, heavy with disappointment, I opened up to Scarlett about my concern.

CHAPTER 23
Joy Story

At that point, Scarlett had moved in, and everything between us was going great. We were building our life together, finding our rhythm, and the last thing I wanted to do was disrupt that harmony. That night, after dinner, I explained my hesitation about bringing Joy to America. I told her why I thought Daniel, despite his young family, should take on the responsibility. She listened intently, her soft brown eyes never leaving mine, and when I finished, she hesitated for only a moment before saying,

"What if we take Joy in?"

Oh, Scarlett—bless her heart! She was so kind, so full of compassion, but also very naïve.

"Scarlett," I said gently, trying to rein in my frustration, "raising a teenager is not what you think. It's complicated, especially a teenage girl. Joy's been through a lot, and this isn't going to be a simple adjustment."

Scarlett's optimism was contagious, even if it was a little misplaced.

"If Joy gets the chance to come to America, it will all be worth it," she said with conviction.

Despite my reservations, I agreed to bring Joy to America. When she arrived, she was bright-eyed and full of excitement, but I could tell there was an undercurrent of nervousness. We immediately got to work, securing a house and enrolling her in the right school. The move was chaotic, but we were determined to give her the best start possible. Scarlett threw herself into the role of caretaker, and for the first few months, things felt manageable.

Scarlett and I were young adults trying to figure out our own lives, yet we were suddenly navigating the uncharted waters of homeownership and parenting a teenage girl. Raising my younger brothers had been hard enough, but Joy wasn't one of the boys—she was sensitive and emotional in ways that made my usual approach to discipline ineffective. I couldn't yell or lay down the law the way I had with my brothers. Every word had to be chosen carefully; every decision weighed against how it might affect her.

Much of the responsibility naturally fell to Scarlett. At 22, she was only eight years older than Joy, and the line between being a sisterly friend and a mother figure blurred daily. Scarlett tried her best to balance the two roles, but it was exhausting. She wanted to be there for Joy, to guide her and support her, but the demands of parenting began to take a toll. Joy needed stability, something Scarlett and I were still learning how to build for ourselves. The strain started to show as Scarlett and I argued more often—sometimes over Joy, sometimes over finances, and sometimes over the fact that we had barely any time for each other. I worried constantly that our decision to bring Joy to America would ultimately hurt our relationship, but every time I saw Joy smile or heard her talk about her dreams, I reminded myself of the reason we did it. Scarlett was right—if Joy could thrive in America, it would all be worth it. Scarlett had signed up for a life with me, not the weight of my family's needs, and I knew it wasn't fair to her. Yet she never complained, at least not in a way that made me doubt her commitment. She was strong in ways I wasn't, and she gave me the strength to keep going. We were learning, making mistakes along the way, but always trying to do right by Joy. Some days were harder than others, but I knew we were doing the best we could. Even though the strain revealed cracks in our relationship, it also showed us the depth of our love and our ability to weather life's storms together. After a year of living with us, Joy began to spiral out of control. She had been abandoned by her father and was living oceans away from her mother. I knew that feeling all too well. I wrestled with the idea of restricting her from speaking to her mother, but I couldn't bring myself to replicate the kind of hurt my father inflicted upon me. Instead, I gently told Joy to give me one more year and fully invest in making things work.

Miraculously, Joy finally started making friends and doing well in school. She was awarded Student of the Month almost every month, and she even became an honor roll student. I couldn't have been prouder, watching her emerge as the brightest of all our siblings.

Throughout the year, Joy continued to thrive. It was as if she had forgotten all about Ghana; her accent had softened, morphing into something closer to that of her white friends. I light-heartedly teased her, calling her "the white girl" whenever she was on the phone. We were all adjusting to our new way of life together as a young family, and one day, Scarlett and I received the incredible news that we were expecting our first baby. We were overjoyed, eagerly planning for the family we had always wanted.

As we prepared for our baby boy's arrival, the spotlight was no longer on Joy, and she felt the shift. She began isolating herself in her room, her grades slipped, and she began losing friends left and right. Her stealing had escalated to the point where Scarlett and I started locking our bedroom door whenever we left her home alone. Each time, it felt like a betrayal—not just of trust, but of the bond we had tried so hard to build with her. It wasn't just about the things she took; it was about what those actions meant, the silent cry for help beneath them.

One evening, after dinner, she came to me with tears in her eyes and confessed. She had stolen a calculator from her teacher. Her voice trembled as she admitted it, and I could see the weight of shame pressed down on her shoulders. I didn't yell. Instead, I asked her to come with me for a drive. She climbed into the car, silent at first, but soon the dam broke. She wept the entire journey, her sobs filling the quiet of the car. Between gasps for air, she cried out for her mother. The pain in her voice was raw, unfiltered, and it cut through me like a knife. My heart broke for her because I recognized that pain—the ache of longing for someone who wasn't there, the confusion and anger of trying to make sense of it all. I wanted to tell her it would get easier, that the hurt would fade, but I knew it wasn't that simple. Instead, I drove and let her cry, hoping the act of being there was enough.

Scarlett and I knew we were in over our heads. Joy's behavior had gone beyond what we could manage on our own. Reluctantly, we sought professional counsel who presented us with a grim diagnosis. Joy's depression had deepened, and her feelings of abandonment were at the root of her struggles. The psychologist's recommendation that it might be best for Joy to return to her mother hit me like a punch to the chest. I fought against the idea, desperate to convince Joy to stay. I reassured her that we loved her, but her longing for home consumed her. She missed her mother, and I couldn't deny her. In a moment of desperation, I called my mother.

Every word Joy had spoken in her tearful outbursts echoed my own feelings from years ago—memories of a childhood spent yearning for the same comfort. I thought my mother would understand, that she'd see Joy's pain, but she refused to take her back. Her voice was firm, almost detached, as she dismissed the idea and tried to redirect the responsibility of caring for Joy to Daniel. Daniel, overwhelmed with the responsibility of expecting his second child, tried to explain his limitations to our mother, but her frustration erupted into anger. She accused Daniel of abandoning the family, failing her, and failing Joy. That heated exchange was the breaking point that marked the beginning of the fractured relationship between Daniel (the quiet one) and our mother. Daniel didn't lash out or argue back; he simply shut down. I could see the weight of it on him, though he never spoke of it again, and he never spoke to my mother again after that. It was a silent wound, that haunted them both. When it was my turn to speak up, emotions harbored since childhood erupted as I screamed into the phone, trembling with rage.

Where were you when we didn't have food to eat?" I shouted, my words sharp and unrelenting. "How could you hand us over to a man like my father? Why didn't you even call us? For eight years, nothing—silence! And the first thing you do when I finally hear from you is ask me for money? I thought you were struggling, but when I came to Ghana, you were doing just fine! The money I sent you—do you know that was all I had to eat? And on top of that, I took care of your son, Daniel! I worried myself sick about him every single day, and now this? Now you're abandoning your own daughter when she needs you the most, just like you abandoned us when we needed you!"

My voice cracked, heavy with years of hurt. Raising your voice to a parent in our culture was unthinkable, yet there I was, breaking that sacred rule. There was silence. Then, a slow, deliberate breath. I expected her to shout, to turn the blame on me. She didn't. Instead, her voice, steady but sorrowful, cut through the silence. "I didn't know. I thought giving you to your father was best. I didn't know he would treat you like that."

I wanted to argue, but the pain in her voice stopped me. Tears fell as my anger gave way to something harder to name—confusion, sorrow, or both.

"He noticed how much you all were struggling to adjust," she continued, her tone thick with regret. "And he decided to cut off our communication. I had no idea..." Her voice broke, and I could hear the tears in her words.

For a moment, neither of us spoke. My chest heaved as I tried to process her explanation. I had spent so many years believing she had abandoned us, that she had chosen her own life over ours. Hearing her regret didn't erase the pain, it complicated it. It was easier to hold onto the story I had told myself for so long, but the reality was that she had also been a victim of my father's choices. My mother believed she was doing what was best for us, but I became more aware of that we were both carrying the weight of a broken past. While her silence had left me to fend for myself, it was clear that her guilt and sorrow had left her just as trapped as I had been. We were confronted with the cost of all our sacrifices.

In a moment that left me utterly stunned, she did something I had never heard an African parent do before—she apologized. "I'm sorry," she said, her voice breaking. "Please forgive me." My anger faltered in the face of her remorse. Although I was still furious with her, the thought of losing my mother was unbearable. She reached out to Daniel, hoping to mend the rift, but the damage was done. Daniel had already shut her out, feeling abandoned by both his parents. Ultimately, we sent Joy back to Ghana and she found her way back to being her joyful self.

CHAPTER 24
Becoming a Father

On a serene Sunday afternoon, a rare moment of calm in our usually busy lives, Scarlett and I took our regular walk around the neighborhood. Our conversations drifted from the future to simple pleasures, the sun casting a warm glow on everything around us. It was one of those perfect days when time seemed to slow down, and everything felt just right. Scarlett suddenly screamed, "Kwasssssi, my water broke!" In an instant, panic surged through me. Without hesitation, I grabbed Scarlett's hands and rushed her to the car. I had always been the cautious driver, until that day. That day, I threw caution to the wind and drove like a man possessed. There was no time to waste. I shifted into overdrive, weaving through traffic with an urgency, each second felt like a lifetime, and I pushed myself to get us to the hospital as quickly as possible.

Watching Scarlett endure the pain of labor, and the way she breathed through each contraction with such determination and resilience left me speechless. The power and grace with which she handled it all was awe-inspiring. I realized then that the strength of a woman went beyond anything I had ever imagined. It was in every breath she took, every push, every moment of struggle; and when she finally gave birth to our beautiful son, I knew I had witnessed something extraordinary.

Leon was born—perfect in every way. He had a full head of dark hair, and when he opened his big brown eyes for the first time, it felt like the world had shifted. Time seemed to pause as I locked eyes with him, and in that moment, the love I felt for him was overwhelming. It was the best feeling I had ever experienced in my life. No achievement, no triumph, could ever compare to the pure joy I felt in that instant. It was a love so deep, so unconditional, that it took my breath away.

Watching Scarlett give birth deepened my love for her. Seeing her strength, her courage, and the way she brought our child into the world, transformed our bond. We had created something so precious that it filled every part of me.

As Leon grew, I began to see the world through his eyes. He showed me more than just the love between Scarlett and me—he revealed the truth about the people around us. Gradually, I lost touch with those who didn't align with the life I was building. Friends and acquaintances I once thought would be lifelong began to fade away. My focus had shifted entirely; Leon had become my everything, and the distractions of the past no longer mattered.

Each day with Leon was a reminder of what truly mattered. His laughter, his milestones, the way he looked at the world with wonder, became my priority. Every moment was a gift, a chance to be the father I had always wanted to be. I was no longer just a man trying to figure out his place in the world; I was a father with a purpose, devoted to cherishing every second of the new chapter in our lives. Excited to welcome another child into our lives, a year and a half later, our sweet Kyrie came into the world. From the moment he was born, it was clear that he had the heart of his mother—gentle, loving, and full of warmth. Yet, despite his soft nature, Kyrie's birth came with its own set of challenges.

Kyrie was born with his umbilical cord wrapped tightly around his neck. As the medical team worked to untangle the cord, I couldn't cut it the way I had with Leon. My heart raced as I watched Kyrie struggle to breathe, his little chest fighting to rise and fall. In that terrifying moment, I felt helpless, more vulnerable than I ever had before. I squeezed Scarlett's hand tightly, whispering reassurances, though I could see the terror mirrored in her eyes. I could feel the weight of the moment—the fear, the uncertainty—and I knew she was just as scared as I was.

Kyrie began to breathe on his own, the tiny sound of his breath filling the room like the sweetest music, but his sugar levels dropped dangerously low, a critical condition that sent us into another whirlwind of tests, monitoring, and prayers. I could hardly sleep, my mind racing with thoughts of what could happen, yet Scarlett and I stood together through it all, leaning on each other for strength. There were moments when the stress felt unbearable, but we never let go of the hope that everything would work out.

After five harrowing days in the hospital, we finally got to bring our baby boy home. I remember holding him for the first time outside the sterile walls of the hospital, breathing in the sweet scent of him, feeling the warmth of his tiny body against mine. It was a relief like no other—our miracle had made it through the storm, and he was finally home.

At first, Leon took his time warming up to Kyrie. He was still our firstborn, the center of our world, and the arrival of a new sibling was a big adjustment for him. But over time, the bond between the two brothers grew stronger. Leon, with his protective nature, began to look out for Kyrie in ways only an older brother could. Kyrie, with his bright eyes and infectious smile, looked up to Leon with complete adoration. They became inseparable, their laughter echoing through our home, a constant reminder of the love that filled every corner of our lives.

Watching them together, I realized that the journey to get where we were had been anything but easy, but every challenge we faced brought us closer. Kyrie's birth tested our strength as parents, but it also deepened our gratitude for the family we had built. It was a love that could withstand anything.

After everything Scarlett and I had endured during Kyrie's birth, we were convinced that our family was complete. We had been through so much already, and the thought of starting over seemed overwhelming. We were finally finding our rhythm with two boys, and life was starting to feel a bit more settled. Shortly after Kyrie's birth, Scarlett developed intense stomach pains, and after a series of tests, the doctor delivered the news that Scarlett had kidney stones that needed to be removed. It was a relief to know what the issue was, and we felt hopeful that it would be a simple procedure, but when the doctors performed the surgery, they didn't find any kidney stones. Instead, they discovered a massive cyst resting on her ovaries. The doctors informed us that she would need another surgery to remove it. We had just gone through so much, and now we were facing yet another challenge.

Two months later, just as we were beginning to breathe a little easier, life threw us another curveball. Scarlett took a pregnancy test on a whim, half-expecting nothing to change. But when the results came back, we were blindsided: she was pregnant again. Our hearts sank as we absorbed the news. We weren't ready for a third baby. Our lives were just starting to settle down. The boys were becoming more independent, and we were finally starting to catch our breath, adjusting to the balance of work, life, and parenting. We had a rhythm, and the thought of disrupting it was overwhelming.

Amid our shock, our reality was clear: You can never question God's plans. Scarlett often said, "I feel like something is missing," and looking back, she was right. There was indeed a void, a space in our family that we hadn't realized was there until our unexpected blessing arrived.

When our baby girl, Nova, was born, everything shifted. It was as if life had finally clicked into place. Holding her in my arms, I felt a love so serene, so calming, and so pure. She brought a sense of peace into our lives that I didn't know we were missing. Her tiny hands wrapped around my finger, and in that moment, I felt a profound connection to her—she was the missing piece.

Nova forced me to rethink my approach to parenting. With Leon and Kyrie, I had always been a protective father, focused on guiding them through their lives with strength and discipline. But with Nova, I found myself embracing a gentler, more nurturing side of myself— one I hadn't fully acknowledged before. She brought out the tenderness in me, and I found joy in just holding her, watching her sleep, and listening to her gentle coos. Parenting her felt different— it felt like a lesson in patience, love, and gentleness. It was as if she had arrived not only to complete our family but to teach me how to be a better father.

With Nova's arrival, our family felt more aligned. The chaos of unexpected turns had led us to a beautiful moment, and as I looked at Scarlett, at the boys, and at Nova, I realized that our family was exactly as it was meant to be. Raising my siblings was a trial, a constant test of patience and resilience, one hardship after another, but it was all preparation. It had all molded me into the father I needed to be. God knew they were more than tests; they were stepping stones that led me to fatherhood. I couldn't help but marvel at how life had come full circle. Ironically, each of my children mirrored a part of my past, a reflection of the people who had shaped me, for better or for worse.

Leon, my oldest, was stubborn and determined. He has that same drive that I saw in my brother, Daniel. He had the same tenacity that made him stand his ground, no matter the odds.

Kyrie, my second son, gentle and loving, exhibited the characteristics of my half-brother, Kenny. His heart open, his love unconditional, and just like Kenny, he could bring peace into any room, finding joy in the simple moments. Watching Kyrie grow was a reminder of the side of me I often buried—the part that yearned for connection, for tenderness, for understanding. Then, there is Nova, our baby girl. From the moment she was born, I could tell she was different. She was strong, independent, and a force to be reckoned with, much like her auntie, Joy. She was already learning to navigate life on her own terms, forging a path that was uniquely hers. In each of my children, I saw my reflection and the echoes of my past. They are my legacy, and in them, I found the meaning of fatherhood. All those years of raising my siblings, the pain and the struggle, had prepared me to be the father I needed to be for them. It wasn't easy, but it was worth it, and I wouldn't trade any of it for the world.

CHAPTER 25
Healing and Forgiveness

Watching my boys shower their sister with love stirred memories of the bond I once shared with my siblings—a bond marked by warmth, protection, and gentle care. I saw Leon's fierce protectiveness and Kyrie's tender comfort in the way they guided Nova, echoing the relationships I once cherished. Yet, over time, that bond had fractured. Distance grew, tensions mounted, and I found myself forced to confront emotional scars I had long ignored—the pain of the scared 10-year-old boy who arrived in America burdened with responsibilities beyond his years.

I realized that in order to heal, I needed to address that past for both my sake and for my children's future. In our culture, therapy was often dismissed as a "white people's thing," something not meant for us, and I had never considered that my struggles with anxiety might stem from that long-ignored trauma. It wasn't until I met Scarlett—who saw the weight I carried and the silent battles I fought—that I began to understand that healing was not a sign of weakness, but a source of strength.

One evening, as Scarlett described how she felt in a stressful situation, her words struck me like a bolt of lightning. I recognized the overwhelming sensation she spoke of—it was all too familiar. Without thinking, I blurted out, "Wow, I know that feeling. That happens to me all the time." She paused, her eyes wide with realization, and simply said, "Kwasi, you have anxiety."

I laughed and brushed it aside. "No, no, Scarlett, black people don't have anxiety," I replied, trying to convince myself more than her. But deep down, something shifted. I realized that all the trauma I had bottled up over the years—years of struggling, of surviving, of always putting others first—was still festering beneath the surface, affecting my every move, my every relationship.

I needed to heal, but pride and stubbornness kept me from seeking therapy. Instead, I prayed—asking for guidance, strength, and the courage to confront the emotional wounds I'd spent years burying. And, as He often does, God, through my prayers, began to show me a path forward.

It was during our estate planning—making arrangements in case something was to happen to us—that I met a lawyer who became a pivotal figure in my life. Rob was a man with over thirty years of experience helping people in the community, someone whose wisdom and kindness had touched many lives. For some reason, in the middle of a conversation, I asked him if I could meet his wife. He looked at me, surprised by the unusual request, but he agreed.

When I met his wife, Julie, I knew my life was about to change. Julie was the epitome of grace and warmth. She walked at least once a day, and, curious about the impact she might have on me, she invited me to join her. The first time I tried to keep up with her, I struggled. She moved with a purpose, a drive that seemed impossible to match. Julie asked about my life, genuinely wanting to know me. She didn't offer advice or try to fix me; she simply listened.

After our first outing, I realized that Julie knew everything about me. Yet, there was no judgment in her gaze. Instead, I saw compassion, understanding, and a deep, motherly love that soothed my weary soul. She embodied the perfect balance of nurturing care and divine wisdom. I started asking her to walk with me once a week, but before I knew it, I was meeting her every day. Each walk became a journey—not just through the neighborhood, but through the corridors of my past. Slowly, Julie helped me extend forgiveness to the 10-year-old boy I had long kept locked away inside.

Before meeting Julie, I often said I had the emotional intelligence of negative one hundred. But she taught me how to open up, how to be vulnerable, and how to face the pain I had buried for so long. Forgiveness was the hardest lesson. I had always believed it was something you gave to others, but Julie helped me see that it was something I needed to give myself. I had to accept that I wasn't perfect—that I was a work in progress and always would be. Through her guidance, I learned to forgive my father, my mother, and, most of all, myself.

The mistakes I made while raising my siblings were many, but they became the lessons that shaped me into the father I am today. It was time to let go of that old role—to release myself from being their father and fully embrace the father my own children needed. That shift wasn't easy, but it was necessary. And as I continued walking with Julie—both literally and metaphorically—I felt the healing begin. It wasn't instantaneous, but with each step, I let go of the past, bit by bit. And with every new day, I grew more ready to embrace the future—one rooted in love, forgiveness, and hope.

Forgiving my father and mother was not an easy thing to do. It felt like a monumental task, one that I wasn't sure I could ever truly accomplish. For years, I held onto so much anger and resentment toward them—anger for the choices they made, for the sacrifices they forced upon us, and for the way they seemed to abandon us when we needed them most. The weight of it all was heavy, and for a long time, I couldn't bring myself to let go of that pain.

But as I worked through my own healing, I realized that I had to put myself in their shoes. I had to understand that their sacrifices, no matter how flawed or misguided, were made out of desperation. They were trying to protect us in the only way they knew how, even if it wasn't the best way. In that realization, I began to see the full picture.

It was through this understanding that I realized my whole life had been spent protecting their sacrifice. I had worked tirelessly, putting my own desires and dreams on hold, trying to ensure that their efforts weren't in vain. And as I saw my siblings grow and succeed—each of them building a life, each of them making something of themselves—I began to see that the sacrifice was not wasted. The sacrifices my parents made, the ones that cost them so much, were worth it because we, their children, were thriving. In their eyes, our success would always be the mark of their success.

I realized that whether I loved or resented my parents, I couldn't change the truth—I would always be Edward and Ama's son. Their blood ran through me, and no matter how far apart we grew, no matter how much pain I held inside, I would always be their child. And in that truth, I found peace. The weight of that was both humbling and freeing. I didn't have to carry the burden of resentment anymore. I could let go of the anger and embrace the reality that their sacrifices had led to something beautiful: our success, our growth, and our ability to build a better life for ourselves and our children.

CHAPTER 26
Discovering Our Bright Future

From an early age, faith shaped my life. After my mother bravely converted from Islam to Christianity, she instilled in us the power of prayer. We fasted with her—though only until noon—always echoing her words: "To gain something, you must sacrifice." At the time, we didn't fully grasp the weight of her teachings; we simply obeyed.

When we arrived in America, my father ordered my two younger brothers and me to attend church every Sunday. Our task was simple, we were to gather as much bread as we could carry home for our family. Once we realized we were just vessels for free food, our attendance dropped. The church began to catch on, and we evaded detection, our cheeks burning with shame. It didn't feel like church; it felt more like stealing. Even though the bread was free, we snuck around to grab it, trying to avoid the shame.

Soccer had introduced me to Jet, a friend who shared my love for God. Jet's father, Pastor Earl, embraced me like family, inviting me to church with open arms. As I began bringing my brothers along, Pastor Earl's warmth enveloped me like a protective blanket. He was always there when I needed guidance. One day, he called with an idea that startled me: a turkey drive to help those in need in Worcester's roughest neighborhoods. It seemed like a reckless venture but swayed by his conviction, I agreed.

We parked on the side of the road, only to find the residents hesitant to approach the "white folks" from the church. It felt like a recipe for disaster. As we hesitated, I overheard hushed voices coming from behind a dumpster. Tension prickled at my skin, but Pastor Earl was unfazed. Suddenly, a man and woman approached us, their eyes glazed, their intentions unclear. Just as I prepared to retreat, a familiar voice broke through the tension: "Kwasi?" It was Maria, my childhood friend! Maria grew up in our Southside neighborhood and was my first friend in America; she was also the first friend whose mother I saw passed out with a needle in her arm. Relief washed over me as we embraced, a moment of warmth amidst uncertainty. She took some turkeys, and together, we distributed the rest to wary residents. Before we parted, we exchanged numbers, and she promised to reconnect soon.

Little did I know that would be our final embrace. Just two months later, a devastating call shattered my world: Maria had overdosed on heroin. The news felt like a punch to the gut. She possessed a heart of gold yet was a casualty of her environment. The "what ifs" haunted me—what if she had been given a better chance? The trauma of her loss settled heavily upon my chest, and vivid nightmares plagued my sleep, where I would confront my fears by praying over the shadows that haunted me. That night, I felt overwhelmed with sadness and helplessness. I prayed to God, asking for guidance. Everything seemed beyond my control, and all I wanted was a chance to help Maria.

The next morning, I woke transformed—an inexplicable joy surged within me. Scarlett looked at me quizzically. "What's gotten into you?" she asked. I could barely contain my excitement: "I understand my purpose." Her brow furrowed, skepticism shadowing her features. I revealed my dream of starting a nonprofit organization to help kids like Maria, to give them the opportunities we had missed. "We'll call it Our Bright Future." Tears filled Scarlett's eyes as she held me close, believing in the vision without hesitation.

I reached out to three friends and shared my plan. Two scoffed and walked away, dismissing my dreams as foolish. But Peter stayed, sharing my conviction. Together with Scarlett, he helped breathe life into our vision. We knocked on countless doors, only to be met with rejection. Yet, in moments of despair, I turned to God for guidance. My prayers were simple, pleading for direction, for Him to use me.

As I moved through networking events, people praised me for the work I was doing for the community. Little did they know, I wasn't the one doing it—this was all God's will. I felt like the biggest beneficiary. The joy I felt from our students' achievements was boundless. They came from diverse backgrounds, but once they joined our program, none of that mattered. They were just kids, immersed in joy, often unaware that their activities were educational. All they cared about was the thrill of watching a robot move or the opportunity to design something special for a loved one.

Among our students, some shared my background, and witnessing their struggles helped me understand them on a profound level. One of them was Jake, a gifted athlete who grappled with academics. When Jake got angry, he was a force of nature—just like I had been on the soccer field. One fateful day, during a basketball game, he lost to his best friend and exploded in frustration. Demanding a rematch, Jake's friend refused, fearing it would only lead to chaos. But Jake wouldn't take no for an answer. He began hurling basketballs around the gym, his fury boiling over.

In a moment of instinct, I rushed in front of him as he grabbed a chair, ready to launch it at anyone nearby. We found ourselves locked in a struggle, the gym now a battleground with just the two of us. I cleared the space, dismissed everyone else, and faced Jake. I understood that his rage wasn't solely about the game; it was a manifestation of deeper wounds. I wrestled the chair from him, as he shouted, "I hate him, I hate him!" Then, the dam broke. Tears streamed down his face as he cried out in despair.

Sitting beside him, I reassured him. "It's okay. You and your best friend will be back playing again tomorrow." But when he looked up at me, he admitted, "It's not my best friend I hate. It's my dad. My mom told me he died, but he's been living in the same town. Why didn't he come to see us?" His father had reappeared after 12 long years, a ghost in Jake's life, and the revelation was like a knife to my heart.

I knew I couldn't help him alone, but I shared what wisdom I could. "I don't know how you feel right now, but you need to be a leader for your sister. Focus on what you can control," I advised. Knowing Jake loved sports, I struck a deal: if he finished his homework, he could have double gym every day. His eyes lit up with determination. From that day forward, he transformed. No longer the boy with Ds and Fs, he began earning Cs and Bs, motivated by the promise of sports. And when I spoke to his mother, we set up therapy. She took the necessary steps to ensure he got the help he needed.

David, another student, almost mirrored my own life. He was always the first to arrive at our program, eager to help clean up. With roots in Ghana, David clung to me because I was the only one who spoke his language. He wore a smile that masked the struggles beneath. His journey to America was fraught with peril that still haunted him.

David and his father embarked on a treacherous journey through Mexico, leaving behind siblings and their mother in search of a better life. They waited for months to cross the border, facing fear and uncertainty. At 1 a.m. on the day they crossed, David woke up, confused and scared. They were packed into a truck, hidden under blankets. "Are we in America?" he whispered to his dad hours later. "Yes, we are, son."

Upon arrival, they rented a single room in a stranger's apartment, David sleeping on a couch. It dawned on me that his eagerness to arrive early stemmed from a fear of missing breakfast. In our program, he found solace in two meals a day, devouring the food others left behind, and saving it for later.

David's passion for soccer mirrored my own. In Ghana, the sport was life, and he dreamed of going pro. One day, while watching him and his friends play, a wave of nostalgia washed over me. But when tensions flared during a game, David's frustration boiled over. He grabbed the ball and declared, "No one can play anymore!" As chaos erupted, I intervened to calm the storm. David was devastated, fearing he might be expelled from the program.

I shared my own struggles with anger, and David's eyes widened as he recognized our shared experiences. He asked questions, and together we navigated the emotions he had long buried. I whispered, "David, remember that anger can signal when it's time to set boundaries and protect yourself. Express it without letting it overwhelm you—use it as a tool for clarity and self-respect." While it was immensely rewarding to support those kids, sometimes the weight of our shared tragedies felt unbearable.

Among all the heart-wrenching stories, Zack's hit me the hardest. He thrived in our digital art program where he created heartfelt messages on shirts. His favorite quote, "It's okay not to be okay," resonated deeply with me. Zack was inclusive, doing exceptionally well, until one day, his father called to say Zack needed a break. He was feeling low, and they would take a week off. I pleaded for Zack to stay, insisting that keeping busy would help. But his dad was firm.

Then, early one Tuesday morning, after dropping my kids off at school, I arrived at the office ready to work. I glanced at my phone and saw a flood of messages. My heart sank as I read an article about a shooting. As I scrolled, my breath hitched. The first victim was Zack's dad. Shock coursed through me, but it only got worse. The second victim was a 14-year-old boy. My heart raced as I read Zack's name.

I had a hard time accepting that it was real. I dug deeper into the news, and there it was, confirming my worst fears: Zack's father's car had been shot twenty-three times. I staggered back in disbelief. *Who could do such a thing?* It was no random act; it was the senseless violence that plagued our streets. My legs buckled beneath me, and I couldn't move. I stepped outside, pacing in despair, tears streaming down my face. The loss felt like losing my own child. For days, I couldn't eat or sleep. All I could do was lie in bed, drowning in grief. The pain was a reminder of the fragility of life and the profound impact these children had on me. Each one held a piece of my heart, and in their struggles, I found my own reflection.

CHAPTER 27
Losing My First Love

Time is a thief, stealing moments we often take for granted. I've spent twenty-four years in America, yet I've only returned to Ghana once. I have three children who have never met my mother, but she made her presence felt every week through FaceTime, speaking to them in our native language. Slowly, my kids picked up a few words, and she delighted in their progress. Nova was her favorite; we named her Nova Ama after my mother. Whenever she FaceTimed, she'd call her friends over to show off her "white grandkids," beaming with pride.

Scarlett and I had planned to visit my mother after her graduation from grad school. It seemed perfect—Scarlett would finish in a year, and we could finally bring the kids to meet their grandmother. One day while driving home from work, an ominous feeling settled in my gut. I called Scarlett, my voice trembling, suggesting I visit my mother sooner with our two boys. "Kwasi, I haven't met her either. I want to meet her too," Scarlett said, making a compelling point. And it felt wrong to rush it.

That Saturday morning, Scarlett was away for her best friend's bachelorette party. It was a rare opportunity for me to spend quality time with the kids. I left my phone in my room, fully engrossed in our little family dance party. Nova's innocent request for a dance party was interrupted by the cold, metallic ring of my phone. I had fifteen missed calls from my brother Daniel, five from my cousin, Blake, and a barrage of missed calls from aunts and uncles back in Ghana. My heart sank—something was terribly wrong.

Blake called again, and I answered.

"Bro, why aren't you picking up your phone?" he demanded. "Our family in Ghana said your mom just died."

The words hit me like a sledgehammer to my chest. I could barely respond. On the other line was my cousin back in Ghana, I picked up his call next. "Is it true?" I asked. He couldn't speak. He just let the weight of his cries wash over me. I couldn't summon tears, but the pain was deep inside. I called Scarlett, my voice breaking, but I urged her not to come home. "I need to hold down the fort," I told myself, using the kids as a shield against my own breakdown.

Time, once our most precious asset, had turned cruel. I couldn't spare two weeks to see my mother while she was alive, yet I was forced to take that time just to say goodbye to her in a casket. Days blurred as friends and family checked in, but I remained unresponsive—a stone wall of grief. Scarlett's constant concern felt suffocating, so I told her to stop.

My relationship with Daniel had soured—we hadn't spoken in over a year. My son Leon mirrored Daniel's negative traits, and it drove me crazy. When I reached out to discuss our travel plans, Daniel kept stalling with excuses like, "Oh bro, I'm working on it." The family back home was waiting for us to finalize our plans so they could set a funeral date, yet Daniel gave me false hope. It broke my heart that even in death, Daniel couldn't forgive our mother.

Our mother had tried reaching out to him for years with no success, and I was saddened by his bitterness and guilt—even when I pleaded with him to join me in Ghana for closure, he continued marching to his own beat. The last time Daniel and I visited our mother was eleven years ago. I once asked her why she never introduced us to her family when we came to Ghana, and she replied, "Not all family members can be trusted."

A week before my departure, my cousin Blake's mother told me to be cautious around family members. "Don't eat any family members' food. Stay in a hotel," she cautioned.

I scoffed; how could I not trust my own family?

On the day I left for Ghana, a tangible dread formed in the pit of my stomach—something I had never experienced before. I had never been away from Scarlett and the kids for any length of time, and we even debated bringing them along. The thought of their first encounter with their grandmother lying in a casket was too much to bear. When I finally landed in Ghana, my cousins welcomed me with a mix of warmth and melancholy. Their familiar faces were bittersweet, each one a reminder of family ties that had been stretched and weathered by time. Through the death of our grandmother, my mother had forced us together under tragic circumstances, there was a certain comfort in reconnecting with relatives. At that moment, amid the grief and the echoes of a past filled with both love and loss, I realized that even in our deepest sorrow, the presence of family could offer solace and a renewed sense of belonging.

The next day, we embarked on a fourteen-hour bus ride back to my hometown. I stared out the window as the landscape blurred by, feeling like a stranger in my own country. When we arrived at my grandmother's house, relatives began filtering in. Familiar yet unfamiliar faces greeted me warmly—and immediately someone asked, "What did you bring me?" I hoped they were joking, but when more pressed the issue, I understood exactly what my mother had feared. Even in our time of grief, her family felt no shame in asking for money.

As my family gathered to discuss the funeral arrangements, they shared disturbing news: my father had claimed responsibility for my mother's death. "I put a curse on her," he had said. In African culture, curses hold immense power, and my family took his words seriously. They rushed from voodoo to voodoo, seeking ways to reverse this supposed curse, despite most of them being Christians who rejected such beliefs. I knew my father craved attention and drama, so I dismissed his claims, focusing on the mourning process instead.

The night before the funeral, my mother's body was brought home, surrounded by her siblings. I couldn't bear to witness it and retreated to my hotel room, where I still hadn't shed a single tear. Ghanaian funerals are week-long events filled with rituals, from the funeral itself to the celebration of life, church services, and yearly commemorations. Each moment is steeped in tradition, cloaked in black and red attire, while black and white are reserved for the celebrations.

Before the guests arrived, our family gathered to view the body. The air was thick with grief, and the scene felt surreal, almost like I was standing outside of myself. My mother lay there, adorned with flowers, her peaceful face surrounded by delicate petals that seemed to honor the life she had lived. Her spirit felt so close as if it was still lingering in the room watching over us. I stood at the back, deliberately holding back, letting the elders go first. I didn't want to rush into this moment, knowing it would be overwhelming.

As I listened to their anguished cries, their voices filled with sorrow, I felt a deep pang of guilt for not having been there when she needed me most. Each cry tore at my soul, but I held everything inside, my emotions threatening to spill over. Finally, after what seemed like an eternity, it was my turn.

I stepped forward, my heart pounding in my chest, my hands trembling as I approached her. She lay there, dressed in a beautiful outfit that seemed to capture the essence of who she was—graceful, kind, and dignified. Seeing her so still made my chest tighten. It was hard to accept that she was really gone. My thoughts raced, and before I knew it, the words escaped me in a whisper: "I'm sorry, Mama, I should've come sooner."

The words hung in the air, heavy with regret. And then, from behind me, I heard my aunts cry out, "Sister Ama, Sister Ama, Paa Kwasi is home!" With the sound of their voices, full of grief, the floodgates opened. All the emotions I had buried for so long came gushing out. I cried, not just for the loss of my mother, but for the years I had spent trying to make sense of a complicated, painful past. My heart shattered as I realized that the woman who had taught me how to love, how to be kind, and how to fight for my family, was no longer here.

In the midst of the tears, I felt a bittersweet sense of peace, as though my mother's love had wrapped itself around me one last time. She may have been gone, but her spirit was with me, in that room, in every tear that fell.

In our tradition, crying is permitted only during the body viewing. As the women stepped away for the casket to be closed, I watched the men from her family prepare to bury her. I stood back, feeling helpless as they lowered her into the ground, the dirt falling over her as if sealing away a part of my soul.

Once the burial was over, we changed into our black and white outfits, ready for the celebration of life. African drums resonated through the night, and we danced, honoring her with joy amidst the sorrow. The following day, at the church service, the pastor spoke of the seasons of life, echoing the truth that life continues regardless of our grief.

Resonating within me, capturing the essence of our existence and offering strength was Ecclesiastes 3:1-8 (King James Version)

To everything there is a season, and a time to every purpose under the heaven:

A time to be born, and a time to die; a time to plant, and a time to pluck up that which is planted; A time to kill, and a time to heal; a time to break down, and a time to build up; A time to weep, and a time to laugh; a time to mourn, and a time to dance; A time to cast away stones, and a time to gather stones together; a time to embrace, and a time to refrain from embracing; A time to get, and a time to lose; a time to keep, and a time to cast away; A time to rend, and a time to sew; a time to keep silence, and a time to speak; A time to love, and a time to hate; a time of war, and a time of peace.

I clung to that scripture as I stood there, overwhelmed by the weight of my loss. The pain of losing my mother felt suffocating, yet within it lay a deeper message—a reminder that life continues even amid sorrow. The words whispered to my heart, assuring me that grief is not an end, but a part of life's cycle. In those verses, I found solace; they acknowledged my pain while inviting me to embrace the enduring beauty of life despite everything.

The funeral was a bittersweet farewell, one filled with both mourning and celebration. It was a journey through grief, but also a journey of gratitude. As I said goodbye to the woman who had shaped me in ways I didn't even fully understand until now, I also celebrated the life she gave me—the sacrifices she made, the lessons she taught, the love she instilled. Her love was like a thread that wove through the fabric of my life, creating the person I had become. She wasn't perfect, but she was mine, and her presence had been a guiding force in my life, even when it felt like I was walking in the dark.

My message to you:

Life is a journey, one that brings moments of joy, moments of sorrow, and everything in between. It's easy to get lost in the chaos, to forget that both the good times and the bad will always pass. The storm will eventually subside, and the sun will rise again. I want you to remember that no matter where you are on your path, time is constantly moving forward, and so will you. The challenges we face today may feel overwhelming, but they too will fade. And the moments of joy and triumph—cherish them, for they, too, are fleeting.

I am grateful for the time you chose to spend it with me, sharing in my story. My hope is that my words resonate with you in a way that brings peace and perspective—helping you navigate the storms of life and appreciate the beauty of the present moment. As Jimi Hendrix once said, "When the power of love overcomes the love of power, the world will know peace." Let that be a guiding light in your journey. Let us all strive for that peace within ourselves, in our relationships, and in the world around us.

About The Author

Author Kwasi Acheampong was born in Ghana, West Africa and moved to the United States of America at the age of 10. His journey, shaped by the challenges and opportunities of immigration, deeply influences his storytelling and fuels his commitment to empowering others. Kwasi is the founder of Our Bright Future, a STEAM-based nonprofit organization dedicated to providing innovative programs such as Robotics, 3D Printing, and Bioscience to local students. As the Executive Director of Our Bright Future, Kwasi is passionate about equipping young minds with the tools and skills to thrive in a rapidly evolving world. A devoted husband to his beloved wife,

Scarlett Acheampong, and a proud father of three amazing children—Leon, Kyrie, and Nova Acheampong. In balancing family, leadership, and service, Kwasi embodies the values of hard work, community, and resilience. Kwasi is a servant to his community and can be reached at info@ourbrightfutureinc.org.